HENRY CABOT LODGE AND THEODORE ROOSEVELT

HERO TALES

FROM

AMERICAN HISTORY

INTRODUCTION BY U.S. SENATOR MITCH McCONNELL
AND GARY L. GREGG II

McConnell Center

Ekstrom Library
University of Louisville
Louisville, Kentucky 40292
(502) 852-8811

www.mcconnellcenter.org

Originally published in 1895

Hence it is that the fathers of these men and ours also, and they themselves likewise, being nurtured in all freedom and well born, have shown before all men many and glorious deeds in public and private, deeming it their duty to fight for the cause of liberty and the Greeks, even against Greeks, and against Barbarians for all the Greeks.

—Plato, "Menexenus."

TO E. Y. R.

To you we owe the suggestion of writing this book. Its purpose, as you know better than any one else, is to tell in simple fashion the story of some Americans who showed that they knew how to live and how to die; who proved their truth by their endeavor; and who joined to the stern and manly qualities which are essential to the well-being of a masterful race the virtues of gentleness, of patriotism, and of lofty adherence to an ideal.

It is a good thing for all Americans, and it is an especially good thing for young Americans, to remember the men who have given their lives in war and peace to the service of their fellow-countrymen, and to keep in mind the feats of daring and personal prowess done in time past by some of the many champions of the nation in the various crises of her history. Thrift, industry, obedience to law, and intellectual cultivation are essential qualities in the makeup of any successful people; but no people can be really great unless they possess also the heroic virtues which are as needful in time of peace as in time of war, and as important in civil as in military life. As a civilized people we desire peace, but the only peace worth having is obtained by instant readiness to fight when wronged—not by unwillingness or inability to fight at all. Intelligent foresight in preparation and known capacity to stand well in battle are the surest safeguards against war. America will cease to be a great nation whenever her young men cease to possess energy, daring, and endurance, as well as the wish and the power to fight the nation's foes. No citizen of a free state should wrong any man; but it is not enough merely to refrain from infringing on the rights of others; he must also be able and willing to stand up for his own rights and those of his country against all comers, and he must be ready at any time to do his full share in resisting either malice domestic or foreign levy.

HENRY CABOT LODGE.
THEODORE ROOSEVELT.
Washington, April 19, 1895.

CONTENTS

Contents

INTRODUCTION

Why hero tales?
Some of us think that heroes, like fairy tales, are only for small children or those who have not yet learned about the "real" world. Others have even told us heroes are unhealthy. Either way, we have all become a bit sheepish about talking of heroes and heroism in America today. Yet virtually every society in history has celebrated its heroes, raising great monuments to their memory; leaving markers along roads where they fell in battle; lavishing praise on them while they lived and creating grand tombs to house them in death. Here in America, it is no different. Almost every town has statues or buildings named after past leaders and monuments commemorating its native sons and daughters who died in battle. How often do we wonder, though, about these people who past generations thought worthy of being followed, remembered and revered?

Have you ever stopped to ask who the man on the horse in the town square was or why he was important? Have you ever paused to read the plaque on the wall of the building that explained its namesake? We have grand national monuments in America as well—the Washington Monument and the Lincoln Memorial, the

Jefferson Memorial and Mount Rushmore come to mind. Do we ever stop to think about why we build them, or what purpose they serve? Whenever we walk around Washington, D.C., it seems we can't go more than a block or two in any direction without running into a memorial dedicated to a military hero or great civilian leader. Why?

Ultimately, what matters are the stories these monuments tell—stories of great individuals doing heroic things that inspire others to do the same. The stories of George Washington, the first hero in this book, inspired the great Kentucky Senator Henry Clay, whose life stories, in turn, inspired Abraham Lincoln, the last hero mentioned in this book. Likewise, Roman heroes like Cato the Younger and Cincinnatus, depicted in popular books and plays of his age, inspired Washington. The stories are what inspire; it is the story that lodges in the imagination of those who hear them, ready to be called up to spark new actions worthy of being called right—and maybe even heroic. That is why Henry Cabot Lodge and Teddy Roosevelt named this little book *Hero Tales from American History*, and that is why they wrote it in the first place.

In the pages that follow, you will read of bloodshed and violence, but you will also read of men risking their lives and fortunes for causes greater than themselves. You will read of men laying down their lives for others. You will read the tale of Daniel Boone and the founding of Kentucky. You will read how Kentucky's own

Introduction

Revolutionary War hero, George Rogers Clark, boldly walked—outnumbered—into an enemy camp and took it without bloodshed. You will read of ships stealthily taken and great battles that raged to change the course of history. You will read about individuals who performed courageous tasks that made America.

When this book was first published, America was only a bit over one hundred years old. Now that we have come more than another century down the road, how many more heroes have we produced? We have been through two great world wars and the Cold War. We have fought in the hot summer jungles and cold winter mountains of Asia. We are fighting now in what has been called a "War on Terror." We have helped liberate people from tyranny, poverty, and hunger and have fought for civil rights. And countless acts of heroism have happened in little towns and big cities when someone quietly accepted the responsibility of serving others, even at great cost to self.

Roosevelt and Lodge primarily picked military heroes as their models. Those are the stories they enjoyed, but they are also the stories which they wanted young people in America to know and be influenced by. Not everyone will appreciate their choices, but no one can deny the importance military heroism has played in defending America and liberating parts of the world. Still, they are not the only heroes worthy of remembrance. As Lodge writes in his essay on the writer Francis Parkman, "Such qualities can be shown in many ways, and the field of battle is only one of the fields of human endeavor where heroism can be displayed."

First published in 1895, there are also no heroines in this book. Many women performed heroic acts before this volume was published and many more since then. Each of us can find many people missing in these pages. That is why we have added a final section to this volume in which we hope you will take time to add heroes and heroines from your own reading and experiences. As Roosevelt and Lodge both knew, heroes and hero tales are essential to inspiring people to be strong, good, true, and courageous when their families, communities and country need them most. We would do well to add to the list that follows the heroes we have encountered or known of in our own lives.

* * *

Teddy Roosevelt and Henry Cabot Lodge were relatively young men with long careers ahead of them when they wrote *Hero Tales from American History.* Lodge was 45 and Roosevelt was 37. They had become friends in Washington, D.C., while Lodge was serving in Congress and Roosevelt was serving on the Civil Service Commission. They spent many hours after dinner talking of great men in American history until Roosevelt's wife suggested one evening that they write down the stories and share them with the country. The two men worked daily with one another on this book until Roosevelt left

Introduction

Washington in early 1895 to become Police Commissioner in New York City.

Both Lodge and Roosevelt wrote numerous books of history and biography during their careers. Lodge would go on to be one of the most important voices related to foreign policy in the early 20th century. He served in the Senate until his death in 1924. Roosevelt went on to live a life worthy of several hero tale entries of his own and served as the 26th president of United States from 1901–1909. His is one of four likenesses on that great wall of heroes we call Mount Rushmore. Neither would deny that the study and the memory of heroes helped to broaden their own horizons and served as models for what they themselves could achieve in life.

Why heroes? That's why.

U.S. SENATOR MITCH MCCONNELL.
GARY L. GREGG II.
Louisville, May 7, 2011.

Hero Tales from American History

WASHINGTON

Hor. *I saw him once; he was a goodly king.*
Ham. *He was a man, take him for all in all, I shall not look upon his like again.*

—HAMLET.

WASHINGTON

The brilliant historian of the English people* has written of Washington, that "no nobler figure ever stood in the fore-front of a nation's life." In any book which undertakes to tell, no matter how slightly, the story of some of the heroic deeds of American history, that noble figure must always stand in the fore-front. But to sketch the life of Washington even in the barest outline is to write the history of the events which made the United States independent and gave birth to the American nation. Even to give a list of what he did, to name his battles and recount his acts as president, would be beyond the limit and the scope of this book. Yet it is always possible to recall the man and to consider what he was and what he meant for us and for mankind. He is worthy the study and the remembrance of all men, and to Americans he is at once a great glory of their past and an inspiration and an assurance of their future.

To understand Washington at all we must first strip off all the myths which have gathered about him. We must cast aside into the dust-heaps all the wretched inventions of the cherry-tree variety, which were fastened upon him

---

* John Richard Green.

nearly seventy years after his birth. We must look at him as he looked at life and the facts about him, without any illusion or deception, and no man in history can better stand such a scrutiny.

Born of a distinguished family in the days when the American colonies were still ruled by an aristocracy, Washington started with all that good birth and tradition could give. Beyond this, however, he had little. His family was poor, his mother was left early a widow, and he was forced after a very limited education to go out into the world to fight for himself. He had strong within him the adventurous spirit of his race. He became a surveyor, and in the pursuit of this profession plunged into the wilderness, where he soon grew to be an expert hunter and backwoodsman. Even as a boy the gravity of his character and his mental and physical vigor commended him to those about him, and responsibility and military command were put in his hands at an age when most young men are just leaving college. As the times grew threatening on the frontier, he was sent on a perilous mission to the Indians, in which, after passing through many hardships and dangers, he achieved success. When the troubles came with France it was by the soldiers under his command that the first shots were fired in the war which was to determine whether the North American continent should be French or English. In his earliest expedition he was defeated by the enemy. Later he was with Braddock, and it was he who tried to rally the broken English army on the stricken field near Fort Duquesne.

On that day of surprise and slaughter he displayed not only cool courage but the reckless daring which was one of his chief characteristics. He so exposed himself that bullets passed through his coat and hat, and the Indians and the French who tried to bring him down thought he bore a charmed life. He afterwards served with distinction all through the French war, and when peace came he went back to the estate which he had inherited from his brother, the most admired man in Virginia.

At that time he married, and during the ensuing years he lived the life of a Virginia planter, successful in his private affairs and serving the public effectively but quietly as a member of the House of Burgesses.

When the troubles with the mother country began to thicken he was slow to take extreme ground, but he never wavered in his belief that all attempts to oppress the colonies should be resisted, and when he once took up his position there was no shadow of turning. He was one of Virginia's delegates to the first Continental Congress, and, although he said but little, he was regarded by all the representatives from the other colonies as the strongest man among them. There was something about him even then which commanded the respect and the confidence of every one who came in contact with him.

It was from New England, far removed from his own State, that the demand came for his appointment as commander-in-chief of the American army.

Silently he accepted the duty, and, leaving Philadelphia, took command of the army at Cambridge. There is no need to trace him through the events that followed. From the time when he drew his sword under the famous elm tree, he was the embodiment of the American Revolution, and without him that revolution would have failed almost at the start. How he carried it to victory through defeat and trial and every possible obstacle is known to all men.

When it was all over he found himself facing a new situation. He was the idol of the country and of his soldiers. The army was unpaid, and the veteran troops, with arms in their hands, were eager to have him take control of the disordered country as Cromwell had done in England a little more than a century before. With the army at his back, and supported by the great forces which, in every community, desire order before everything else, and are ready to assent to any arrangement which will bring peace and quiet, nothing would have been easier than for Washington to have made himself the ruler of the new nation. But that was not his conception of duty, and he not only refused to have anything to do with such a movement himself, but he repressed, by his dominant personal influence, all such intentions on the part of the army. On the 23rd of December, 1783, he met the Congress at Annapolis, and there resigned his commission. What he then said is one of the two most memorable speeches ever made in the United States, and is also memorable for its meaning and spirit among all speeches ever made by men. He spoke as follows:

Mr. President:—The great events on which my resignation depended having at length taken place, I have now the honor of offering my sincere congratulations to Congress, and of presenting myself before them, to surrender into their hands the trust committed to me and to claim the indulgence of retiring from the service of my country.

Happy in the confirmation of our independence and sovereignty and pleased with the opportunity afforded the United States of becoming a respectable nation, I resign with satisfaction the appointment I accepted with diffidence; a diffidence in my abilities to accomplish so arduous a task, which, however, was superseded by a confidence in the rectitude of our cause, the support of the supreme power of the Union, and the patronage of Heaven.

The successful termination of the war has verified the most sanguine expectations, and my gratitude for the interposition of Providence and the assistance I have received from my countrymen increases with every review of the momentous contest.

While I repeat my obligations to the Army in general, I should do injustice to my own feelings not to acknowledge, in this place, the peculiar services and distinguished merits of the Gentlemen who have been attached to my person during the war. It was impossible that the choice of confidential officers to compose my family should have been more fortunate. Permit me, sir, to recommend in particular those who have continued in service to the present moment as worthy of the favorable notice and patronage of Congress.

I consider it an indispensable duty to close this last solemn act of my official life by commending the interests of our dearest country to the protection of Almighty God, and those who have the superintendence of them to His holy keeping.

Having now finished the work assigned me, I retire from the great theatre of action, and, bidding an affectionate farewell to this august body, under whose orders I have so long acted, I here offer my commission and take my leave of all the employments of public life.

The great master of English fiction, writing of this scene at Annapolis, says: "Which was the most splendid spectacle ever witnessed—the opening feast of Prince George in London, or the resignation of Washington? Which is the noble character for after ages to admire—yon fribble dancing in lace and spangles, or yonder hero who sheathes his sword after a life of spotless honor, a purity unreproached, a courage indomitable and a consummate victory?"

Washington did not refuse the dictatorship, or, rather, the opportunity to take control of the country, because he feared heavy responsibility, but solely because, as a high-minded and patriotic man, he did not believe in meeting the situation in that way. He was, moreover, entirely devoid of personal ambition, and had no vulgar longing for personal power. After resigning his commission he returned quietly to Mount Vernon, but he did not hold himself aloof from public affairs. On the contrary, he watched their course with the utmost anxiety. He saw the feeble Confederation breaking to pieces, and he soon realized that that form of government was an utter failure. In a time when no American statesman except Hamilton had yet freed himself from the local feelings of the colonial days, Washington was thoroughly national in all his views. Out of the thirteen jarring colonies he meant that a nation should come, and he saw—what no one else saw—the destiny of the country to the westward. He wished a nation founded which should cross the Alleghanies, and, holding the mouths of the Mississippi, take possession of all that vast and then unknown region. For these reasons he stood at the head of the national movement, and to him all men turned who desired a better union and sought to bring order out of chaos. With him Hamilton and Madison consulted in the preliminary stages which were to lead to the formation of a new system. It was his vast personal influence which made that movement a success, and when the convention to form a constitution met at Philadelphia, he presided over its deliberations, and it was his commanding will which, more than anything else, brought a constitution through difficulties and conflicting interests which more than once made any result seem well-nigh hopeless.

When the Constitution formed at Philadelphia had

been ratified by the States, all men turned to Washington to stand at the head of the new government. As he had borne the burden of the Revolution, so he now took up the task of bringing the government of the Constitution into existence. For eight years he served as president. He came into office with a paper constitution, the heir of a bankrupt, broken-down confederation. He left the United States, when he went out of office, an effective and vigorous government. When he was inaugurated, we had nothing but the clauses of the Constitution as agreed to by the Convention. When he laid down the presidency, we had an organized government, an established revenue, a funded debt, a high credit, an efficient system of banking, a strong judiciary, and an army. We had a vigorous and well-defined foreign policy; we had recovered the western posts, which, in the hands of the British, had fettered our march to the west; and we had proved our power to maintain order at home, to repress insurrection, to collect the national taxes, and to enforce the laws made by Congress. Thus Washington had shown that rare combination of the leader who could first destroy by revolution, and who, having led his country through a great civil war, was then able to build up a new and lasting fabric upon the ruins of a system which had been overthrown.

At the close of his official service he returned again to Mount Vernon, and, after a few years of quiet retirement, died just as the century in which he had played so great a part was closing.

Washington stands among the greatest men of human

history, and those in the same rank with him are very few. Whether measured by what he did, or what he was, or by the effect of his work upon the history of mankind, in every aspect he is entitled to the place he holds among the greatest of his race. Few men in all time have such a record of achievement.

Still fewer can show at the end of a career so crowded with high deeds and memorable victories a life so free from spot, a character so unselfish and so pure, a fame so void of doubtful points demanding either defense or explanation. Eulogy of such a life is needless, but it is always important to recall and to freshly remember just what manner of man he was.

In the first place he was physically a striking figure. He was very tall, powerfully made, with a strong, handsome face. He was remarkably muscular and powerful. As a boy he was a leader in all outdoor sports. No one could fling the bar further than he, and no one could ride more difficult horses. As a young man he became a woodsman and hunter. Day after day he could tramp through the wilderness with his gun and his surveyor's chain, and then sleep at night beneath the stars.

He feared no exposure or fatigue, and outdid the hardiest backwoodsman in following a winter trail and swimming icy streams. This habit of vigorous bodily exercise he carried through life. Whenever he was at Mount Vernon he gave a large part of his time to fox-hunting, riding after his hounds through the most difficult country. His physical power and endurance counted for much in his success when he commanded his army, and when the heavy anxieties of general and president weighed upon his mind and heart.

He was an educated, but not a learned man. He read well and remembered what he read, but his life was, from the beginning, a life of action, and the world of men was his school. He was not a military genius like Hannibal, or Caesar, or Napoleon, of which the world has had only three or four examples. But he was a great soldier of the type which the English race has produced, like Marlborough and Cromwell, Wellington, Grant, and Lee. He was patient under defeat, capable of large combinations, a stubborn and often reckless fighter, a winner of battles, but much more, a conclusive winner in a long war of varying fortunes. He was, in addition, what very few great soldiers or commanders have ever been, a great constitutional statesman, able to lead a people along the paths of free government without undertaking himself to play the part of the strong man, the usurper, or the savior of society.

He was a very silent man. Of no man of equal importance in the world's history have we so few sayings of a personal kind. He was ready enough to talk or to write about the public duties which he had in hand, but he hardly ever talked of himself. Yet there can be no greater error than to suppose Washington cold and unfeeling, because of his silence and reserve. He was by nature a man of strong desires and stormy passions. Now and again he would break out, even as late as the presidency, into a gust of anger that would sweep everything before it. He was always reckless of personal danger, and had a fierce fighting spirit which nothing could check when it was once unchained.

But as a rule these fiery impulses and strong passions were under the absolute control of an iron will, and they never clouded his judgment or warped his keen sense of justice.

But if he was not of a cold nature, still less was he hard or unfeeling. His pity always went out to the poor, the oppressed, or the unhappy, and he was all that was kind and gentle to those immediately about him.

We have to look carefully into his life to learn all these things, for the world saw only a silent, reserved man, of courteous and serious manner, who seemed to stand alone and apart, and who impressed every one who came near him with a sense of awe and reverence.

One quality he had which was, perhaps, more characteristic of the man and his greatness than any other. This was his perfect veracity of mind.

He was, of course, the soul of truth and honor, but he was even more than that. He never deceived himself. He always looked facts squarely in the face and dealt with them as such, dreaming no dreams, cherishing no delusions, asking no impossibilities,—just to others as to himself, and thus winning alike in war and in peace.

He gave dignity as well as victory to his country and his cause. He was, in truth, a "character for after ages to admire."

DANIEL BOONE
AND THE
FOUNDING OF
KENTUCKY

. . . Boone lived hunting up to ninety;

And, what's still stranger, left behind a name
    For which men vainly decimate the throng,
Not only famous, but of that GOOD fame,
    Without which glory's but a tavern song,—
Simple, serene, the antipodes of shame,
    Which hate nor envy e'er could tinge with wrong;

'T is true he shrank from men, even of his nation;
    When they built up unto his darling trees,
He moved some hundred miles off, for a station
    Where there were fewer houses and more ease;

      * * *

But where he met the individual man,
He showed himself as kind as mortal can.

      * * *

The freeborn forest found and kept them free,
And fresh as is a torrent or a tree.

And tall, and strong, and swift of foot were they,
    Beyond the dwarfing city's pale abortions,
Because their thoughts had never been the prey
    Of care or gain; the green woods were their portions

      * * *

Simple they were, not savage; and their rifles,
Though very true, were yet not used for trifles.

      * * *

Serene, not sullen, were the solitudes
Of this unsighing people of the woods.

                       —BYRON.

DANIEL BOONE AND THE FOUNDING OF KENTUCKY

D aniel Boone will always occupy a unique place
in our history as the archetype of the hunter and
wilderness wanderer. He was a true pioneer, and stood
at the head of that class of Indian-fighters, game-hunters,
forest-fellers, and backwoods farmers who, generation
after generation, pushed westward the border of civilization from the Alleghanies to the Pacific. As he himself
said, he was "an instrument ordained of God to settle
the wilderness." Born in Pennsylvania, he drifted south
into western North Carolina, and settled on what was
then the extreme frontier. There he married, built a log
cabin, and hunted, chopped trees, and tilled the ground
like any other frontiersman. The Alleghany Mountains
still marked a boundary beyond which the settlers dared
not go; for west of them lay immense reaches of frowning
forest, uninhabited save by bands of warlike Indians.
Occasionally some venturesome hunter or trapper
penetrated this immense wilderness, and returned with
strange stories of what he had seen and done.

In 1769 Boone, excited by these vague and wondrous
tales, determined himself to cross the mountains and find

out what manner of land it was that lay beyond. With a few chosen companions he set out, making his own trail through the gloomy forest. After weeks of wandering, he at last emerged into the beautiful and fertile country of Kentucky, for which, in after years, the red men and the white strove with such obstinate fury that it grew to be called "the dark and bloody ground." But when Boone first saw it, it was a fair and smiling land of groves and glades and running waters, where the open forest grew tall and beautiful, and where innumerable herds of game grazed, roaming ceaselessly to and fro along the trails they had trodden during countless generations. Kentucky was not owned by any Indian tribe, and was visited only by wandering war-parties and hunting-parties who came from among the savage nations living north of the Ohio or south of the Tennessee.

A roving war-party stumbled upon one of Boone's companions and killed him, and the others then left Boone and journeyed home; but his brother came out to join him, and the two spent the winter together.

Self-reliant, fearless, and the frowning defiles of Cumberland Gap, they were attacked by Indians, and driven back—two of Boone's own sons being slain. In 1775, however, he made another attempt; and this attempt was successful. The Indians attacked the newcomers; but by this time the parties of would-be settlers were sufficiently numerous to hold their own. They beat back the Indians, and built rough little hamlets, surrounded by log stockades, at Boonesborough and Harrodsburg; and the permanent settlement of Kentucky had begun.

The next few years were passed by Boone amid unending Indian conflicts.

He was a leader among the settlers, both in peace and in war. At one time he represented them in the House of Burgesses of Virginia; at another time he was a member of the first little Kentucky parliament itself; and he became a colonel of the frontier militia. He tilled the land, and he chopped the trees himself; he helped to build the cabins and stockades with his own hands, wielding the longhandled, light-headed frontier ax as skilfully as other frontiersmen. His main business was that of surveyor, for his knowledge of the country, and his ability to travel through it, in spite of the danger from Indians, created much demand for his services among people who wished to lay off tracts of wild land for their own future use. But whatever he did, and wherever he went, he had to be sleeplessly on the lookout for his Indian foes. When he and his fellows tilled the stump-dotted fields of corn, one or more of the party were always on guard, with weapon at the ready, for fear of lurking savages. When he went to the House of Burgesses he carried his long rifle, and traversed roads not a mile of which was free from the danger of Indian attack. The settlements in the early years depended exclusively upon game for their meat, and Boone was the mightiest of all the hunters, so that upon him devolved the task of keeping his people supplied.

He killed many buffaloes, and pickled the buffalo beef for use in winter. He killed great numbers of black bear, and made bacon of them, precisely as if they had been hogs. The common game were deer and elk. At that time none of the hunters of Kentucky would waste a shot on anything so small as a prairie-chicken or wild duck; but they sometimes killed geese and swans when they came south in winter and lit on the rivers.

But whenever Boone went into the woods after game, he had perpetually to keep watch lest he himself might be hunted in turn. He never lay in wait at a game-lick, save with ears strained to hear the approach of some crawling red foe. He never crept up to a turkey he heard calling, without exercising the utmost care to see that it was not an Indian; for one of the favorite devices of the Indians was to imitate the turkey call, and thus allure within range some inexperienced hunter.

Besides this warfare, which went on in the midst of his usual vocations, Boone frequently took the field on set expeditions against the savages.

Once when he and a party of other men were making salt at a lick, they were surprised and carried off by the Indians. The old hunter was a prisoner with them for some months, but finally made his escape and came home through the trackless woods as straight as the wild pigeon flies.

He was ever on the watch to ward off the Indian inroads, and to follow the warparties, and try to rescue the prisoners. Once his own daughter, and two other girls who were with her, were carried off by a band of Indians. Boone raised some friends and followed the trail steadily for two days and a night; then they came to where the Indians had killed a buffalo calf and were camped around it. Firing from a little distance, the whites shot two of the Indians, and, rushing in, rescued the girls.

On another occasion, when Boone had gone to visit a salt-lick with his brother, the Indians ambushed them and shot the latter. Boone himself escaped, but the Indians followed him for three miles by the aid of a tracking dog, until Boone turned, shot the dog, and then eluded his pursuers. In company with Simon Kenton and many other noted hunters and wilderness warriors, he once and again took part in expeditions into the Indian country, where they killed the braves and drove off the horses.

Twice bands of Indians, accompanied by French, Tory, and British partizans from Detroit, bearing the flag of Great Britain, attacked Boonesboroug. In each case Boone and his fellow-settlers beat them off with loss. At the fatal battle of the Blue Licks, in which two hundred of the best riflemen of Kentucky were beaten with terrible slaughter by a great force of Indians from the lakes, Boone commanded the left wing.

Leading his men, rifle in hand, he pushed back and overthrew the force against him; but meanwhile the Indians destroyed the right wing and center, and got round in his rear, so that there was nothing left for Boone's men except to flee with all possible speed.

As Kentucky became settled, Boone grew restless and ill at ease.

He loved the wilderness; he loved the great forests and the great prairie-like glades, and the life in the little lonely cabin, where from the door he could see the deer come out into the clearing at nightfall.

The neighborhood of his own kind made him feel cramped and ill at ease.

So he moved ever westward with the frontier; and as Kentucky filled up he crossed the Mississippi and settled on the borders of the prairie country of Missouri, where the Spaniards, who ruled the territory, made him an alcalde, or judge. He lived to a great age, and died out on the border, a backwoods hunter to the last.

GEORGE ROGERS CLARK AND THE CONQUEST OF THE NORTHWEST

Have the elder races halted?
Do they droop and end their lesson, wearied over there beyond
the seas?
We take up the task eternal, and the burden and the lesson,
Pioneers! O Pioneers!
All the past we leave behind,
We debouch upon a newer, mightier world, varied world;
Fresh and strong the world we seize, world of labor and the
march,
Pioneers! O Pioneers!
We detachments steady throwing,
Down the edges, through the passes, up the mountains steep,
Conquering, holding, daring, venturing, as we go the
unknown ways,
Pioneers! O Pioneers!

* * *

The sachem blowing the smoke first towards the sun and then
towards the earth,
The drama of the scalp dance enacted with painted faces and
guttural exclamations,
The setting out of the war-party, the long and stealthy march,
The single file, the swinging hatchets, the surprise and
slaughter of enemies.

—WHITMAN.

GEORGE ROGERS CLARK AND THE CONQUEST OF THE NORTHWEST

In 1776, when independence was declared, the United States included only the thirteen original States on the seaboard. With the exception of a few hunters there were no white men west of the Alleghany Mountains, and there was not even an American hunter in the great country out of which we have since made the States of Illinois, Indiana, Ohio, Michigan, and Wisconsin. All this region north of the Ohio River then formed apart of the Province of Quebec. It was a wilderness of forests and prairies, teeming with game, and inhabited by many warlike tribes of Indians.

Here and there through it were dotted quaint little towns of French Creoles, the most important being Detroit, Vincennes on the Wabash, and Kaskaskia and Kahokia on the Illinois. These French villages were ruled by British officers commanding small bodies of regular soldiers or Tory rangers and Creole partizans. The towns were completely in the power of the British government;

none of the American States had actual possession of a foot of property in the Northwestern Territory.

The Northwest was acquired in the midst of the Revolution only by armed conquest, and if it had not been so acquired, it would have remained a part of the British Dominion of Canada.

The man to whom this conquest was clue was a famous backwoods leader, a mighty hunter, a noted Indian-fighter, George Rogers Clark. He was a very strong man, with light hair and blue eyes. He was of good Virginian family. Early in his youth, he embarked on the adventurous career of a backwoods surveyor, exactly as Washington and so many other young Virginians of spirit did at that period. He traveled out to Kentucky soon after it was founded by Boone, and lived there for a year, either at the stations or camping by him self in the woods, surveying, hunting, and making war against the Indians like any other settler; but all the time his mind was bent on vaster schemes than were dreamed of by the men around him. He had his spies out in the Northwestern Territory, and became convinced that with a small force of resolute backwoodsmen he could conquer it for the United States. When he went back to Virginia, Governor Patrick Henry entered heartily into Clark's schemes and gave him authority to fit out a force for his purpose.

In 1778, after encountering endless difficulties and delays, he finally raised a hundred and fifty backwoods riflemen. In May they started down the Ohio in flatboats to undertake the allotted task. They drifted and rowed downstream to the Falls of the Ohio, where Clark founded a log hamlet, which has since become the great city of Louisville.

Here he halted for some days and was joined by fifty or sixty volunteers; but a number of the men deserted, and when, after an eclipse of the sun, Clark again pushed off to go down with the current, his force was but about one hundred and sixty riflemen. All, however, were men on whom he could depend—men well used to frontier warfare. They were tall, stalwart backwoodsmen, clad in the hunting-shirt and leggings that formed the national dress of their kind, and armed with the distinctive weapon of the backwoods, the long-barreled, small-bore rifle.

Before reaching the Mississippi the little flotilla landed, and Clark led his men northward against the Illinois towns. In one of them, Kaskaskia, dwelt the British commander of the entire district up to Detroit. The small garrison and the Creole militia taken together outnumbered Clark's force, and they were in close alliance with the Indians roundabout. Clark was anxious to take the town by surprise and avoid bloodshed, as he believed he could win over the Creoles to the American side. Marching cautiously by night and generally hiding by day, he came to the outskirts of the little village on the evening of July 4, and lay in the woods near by until after nightfall.

Fortune favored him. That evening the officers of the garrison had given a great ball to the mirth-loving

Creoles, and almost the entire population of the village had gathered in the fort, where the dance was held. While the revelry was at its height, Clark and his tall backwoodsmen, treading silently through the darkness, came into the town, surprised the sentries, and surrounded the fort without causing any alarm.

All the British and French capable of bearing arms were gathered in the fort to take part in or look on at the merrymaking. When his men were posted Clark walked boldly forward through the open door, and, leaning against the wall, looked at the dancers as they whirled around in the light of the flaring torches. For some moments no one noticed him.

Then an Indian who had been lying with his chin on his hand, looking carefully over the gaunt figure of the stranger, sprang to his feet, and uttered the wild war-whoop. Immediately the dancing ceased and the men ran to and fro in confusion; but Clark, stepping forward, bade them be at their ease, but to remember that henceforth they danced under the flag of the United States, and not under that of Great Britain.

The surprise was complete, and no resistance was attempted. For twenty-four hours the Creoles were in abject terror. Then Clark summoned their chief men together and explained that he came as their ally, and not as their foe, and that if they would join with him they should be citizens of the American republic, and treated in all respects on an equality with their comrades. The Creoles, caring little for the British, and rather fickle of nature, accepted the proposition with joy, and with the most enthusiastic loyalty toward Clark. Not only that, but sending messengers to their kinsmen on the Wabash, they persuaded the people of Vincennes likewise to cast off their allegiance to the British king, and to hoist the American flag.

So far, Clark had conquered with greater ease than he had dared to hope.

But when the news reached the British governor, Hamilton, at Detroit, he at once prepared to reconquer the land. He had much greater forces at his command than Clark had; and in the fall of that year he came down to Vincennes by stream and portage, in a great fleet of canoes bearing five hundred fighting men—British regulars, French partizans, and Indians.

The Vincennes Creoles refused to fight against the British, and the American officer who had been sent thither by Clark had no alternative but to surrender.

If Hamilton had then pushed on and struck Clark in Illinois, having more than treble Clark's force, he could hardly have failed to win the victory; but the season was late and the journey so difficult that he did not believe it could be taken. Accordingly he disbanded the Indians and sent some of his troops back to Detroit, announcing that when spring came he would march against Clark in Illinois.

If Clark in turn had awaited the blow he would have surely met defeat; but he was a greater man than his antagonist, and he did what the other deemed impossible.

Finding that Hamilton had sent home some of his troops and dispersed all his Indians, Clark realized that his chance was to strike before Hamilton's soldiers assembled again in the spring. Accordingly he gathered together the pick of his men, together with a few Creoles, one hundred and seventy all told, and set out for Vincennes. At first the journey was easy enough, for they passed across the snowy Illinois prairies, broken by great reaches of lofty woods. They killed elk, buffalo, and deer for food, there being no difficulty in getting all they wanted to eat; and at night they built huge fires by which to sleep, and feasted "like Indian war-dancers," as Clark said in his report.

But when, in the middle of February, they reached the drowned lands of the Wabash, where the ice had just broken up and everything was flooded, the difficulties seemed almost insuperable, and the march became painful and laborious to a degree. All day long the troops waded in the icy water, and at night they could with difficulty find some little hillock on which to sleep. Only Clark's indomitable courage and cheerfulness kept the party in heart and enabled them to persevere. However, persevere they did, and at last, on February 23, they came in sight of the town of Vincennes. They captured a Creole who was out shooting ducks, and from him learned that their approach was utterly unsuspected, and that there were many Indians in town.

Clark was now in some doubt as to how to make his fight. The British regulars dwelt in a small fort at one end of the town, where they had two light guns; but Clark feared lest, if he made a sudden night attack, the townspeople and Indians would from sheer fright turn against him. He accordingly arranged, just before he himself marched in, to send in the captured duck-hunter, conveying a warning to the Indians and the Creoles that he was about to attack the town, but that his only quarrel was with the British, and that if the other inhabitants would stay in their own homes they would not be molested. Sending the duck-hunter ahead, Clark took up his march and entered the town just after nightfall. The news conveyed by the released hunter astounded the townspeople, and they talked it over eagerly, and were in doubt what to do. The Indians, not knowing how great might be the force that would assail the town, at once took refuge in the neighboring woods, while the Creoles retired to their own houses. The British knew nothing of what had happened until the Americans had actually entered the streets of the little village.

Rushing forward, Clark's men soon penned the regulars within their fort, where they kept them surrounded all night. The next day a party of Indian warriors, who in the British interest had been ravaging the settlements of Kentucky, arrived and entered the town, ignorant that the Americans had captured it. Marching boldly forward to the fort, they suddenly found it beleaguered, and before they could flee they were seized by the backwoodsmen. In their belts they carried the scalps of the slain settlers. The savages were taken redhanded, and the American frontiersmen were in no mood to show mercy. All the Indians were tomahawked in sight of the fort.

For some time the British defended themselves well; but at length their guns were disabled, all of the gunners being picked off by the backwoods marksmen, and finally the garrison dared not so much as appear at a port-hole, so deadly was the fire from the long rifles. Under such circumstances Hamilton was forced to surrender.

No attempt was afterward made to molest the Americans in the land they had won, and upon the conclusion of peace the Northwest, which had been conquered by Clark, became part of the United States.

THE BATTLE
OF TRENTON

And such they are—and such they will be found:
Not so Leonidas and Washington,
Their every battle-field is holy ground
Which breathes of nations saved, not worlds undone.
How sweetly on the ear such echoes sound!
While the mere victor's may appal or stun
The servile and the vain, such names will be
A watchword till the future shall be free.

—BYRON.

THE BATTLE OF TRENTON

In December, 1776, the American Revolution was at its lowest ebb. The first burst of enthusiasm, which drove the British back from Concord and met them hand to hand at Bunker Hill, which forced them to abandon Boston and repulsed their attack at Charleston, had spent its force. The undisciplined American forces called suddenly from the workshop and the farm had given way, under the strain of a prolonged contest, and had been greatly scattered, many of the soldiers returning to their homes.

The power of England, on the other hand, with her disciplined army and abundant resources, had begun to tell. Washington, fighting stubbornly, had been driven during the summer and autumn from Long Island up the Hudson, and New York had passed into the hands of the British. Then Forts Lee and Washington had been lost, and finally the Continental army had retreated to New Jersey. On the second of December Washington was at Princeton with some three thousand ragged soldiers, and had escaped destruction only by the rapidity of his movements. By the middle of the month General Howe felt that the American army, unable as he believed either to fight or to withstand the winter, must soon dissolve, and, posting strong detachments at various points, he took up his winter quarters in New York. The British general had under his command in his various divisions twenty-five thousand well-disciplined soldiers, and the conclusion he had reached was not an unreasonable one; everything, in fact, seemed to confirm his opinion. Thousands of the colonists were coming in and accepting his amnesty. The American militia had left the field, and no more would turn out, despite Washington's earnest appeals.

All that remained of the American Revolution was the little Continental army and the man who led it.

Yet even in this dark hour Washington did not despair. He sent in every direction for troops. Nothing was forgotten. Nothing that he could do was left undone. Unceasingly he urged action upon Congress, and at the same time with indomitable fighting spirit he planned to attack the British. It was a desperate undertaking in the face of such heavy odds, for in all his divisions he had only some six thousand men, and even these were scattered. The single hope was that by his own skill and courage he could snatch victory from a situation where victory seemed impossible. With the instinct of a great commander he saw that his only chance was to fight the British detachments suddenly, unexpectedly, and separately, and to do this not only required secrecy and perfect judgment, but also the cool, unwavering courage of which, under such circumstances, very few men have proved themselves capable. As Christmas approached his plans were ready. He determined to fall upon the British detachment of Hessians, under Colonel Rahl, at Trenton, and there strike his first blow. To each division of his little army a part in the attack was assigned with careful forethought. Nothing was overlooked and nothing omitted, and then, for some reason good or bad, every one of the division commanders failed to do his part. As the general plan was arranged, Gates was to march from Bristol with two thousand men; Ewing was to cross at Trenton; Putnam was to come up from Philadelphia; and Griffin was to make a diversion against Donop. When the moment came, Gates, who disapproved the plan, was on his way to Congress; Griffin abandoned New Jersey and fled before Donop; Putnam did not attempt to leave Philadelphia; and Ewing made no effort to cross at Trenton.

Cadwalader came down from Bristol, looked at the river and the floating ice, and then gave it up as desperate. Nothing remained except Washington himself with the main army, but he neither gave up, nor hesitated, nor stopped on account of the ice, or the river, or the perils which lay beyond. On Christmas Eve, when all the Christian world was feasting and rejoicing, and while the British were enjoying themselves in their comfortable quarters, Washington set out. With twenty-four hundred men he crossed the Delaware through the floating ice, his boats managed and rowed by the sturdy fishermen of Marblehead from Glover's regiment. The crossing was successful, and he landed about nine miles from Trenton.

It was bitter cold, and the sleet and snow drove sharply in the faces of the troops. Sullivan, marching by the river, sent word that the arms of his soldiers were wet. "Tell your general," was Washington's reply to the message, "to use the bayonet, for the town must be taken." When they reached Trenton it was broad daylight.

Washington, at the front and on the right of the line, swept down the Pennington road, and, as he drove back the Hessian pickets, he heard the shout of Sullivan's men as, with Stark leading the van, they charged in from the river. A company of jaegers and of light dragoons slipped away.

There was some fighting in the streets, but the attack was so strong and well calculated that resistance was useless. Colonel Rahl, the British commander, aroused from his revels, was killed as he rushed out to rally his men, and in a few moments all was over. A thousand prisoners fell into Washington's hands, and this important detachment of the enemy was cut off and destroyed.

The news of Trenton alarmed the British, and Lord Cornwallis with seven thousand of the best troops started at once from New York in hot pursuit of the American army. Washington, who had now rallied some five thousand men, fell back, skirmishing heavily, behind the Assunpink, and when Cornwallis reached the river he found the American army awaiting him on the other side of the stream. Night was falling, and Cornwallis, feeling sure of his prey, decided that he would not risk an assault until the next morning. Many lessons had not yet taught him that it was a fatal business to give even twelve hours to the great soldier opposed to him.

During the night Washington, leaving his fires burning and taking a roundabout road which he had already reconnoitered, marched to Princeton. There he struck another British detachment. A sharp fight ensued, the British division was broken and defeated, losing some five hundred men, and Washington withdrew after this second victory to the highlands of New Jersey to rest and recruit.

Frederick the Great is reported to have said that this was the most brilliant campaign of the century. With a force very much smaller than that of the enemy, Washington had succeeded in striking the British at two places with superior forces at each point of contact. At Trenton he had the benefit of a surprise, but the second time he was between two hostile armies. He was ready to fight Cornwallis when the latter reached the Assunpink, trusting to the strength of his position to make up for his inferiority of numbers. But when Cornwallis gave him the delay of a night, Washington, seeing the advantage offered by his enemy's mistake, at once changed his whole plan, and, turning in his tracks, fell upon the smaller of the two forces opposed to him, wrecking and defeating it before the outgeneraled Cornwallis could get up with the main army.

Washington had thus shown the highest form of military skill, for there is nothing that requires so much judgment and knowledge, so much certainty of movement and quick decision, as to meet a superior enemy at different points, force the fighting, and at each point to outnumber and overwhelm him.

But the military part of this great campaign was not all. Many great soldiers have not been statesmen, and have failed to realize the political necessities of the situation. Washington presented the rare combination of a great soldier and a great statesman as well. He aimed not only to win battles, but by his operations in the field to influence the political situation and affect public opinion. The American Revolution was going to pieces. Unless some decisive victory could be won immediately, it would have come to an end in the winter of 1776–77.

This Washington knew, and it was this which nerved his arm. The results justified his forethought. The victories of Trenton and Princeton restored the failing spirits of the people, and, what was hardly less important, produced a deep impression in Europe in favor of the colonies. The country, which had lost heart, and become supine and almost hostile, revived. The militia again took the field. Outlying parties of the British were attacked and cut off, and recruits once more began to come in to the Continental army. The Revolution was saved. That the English colonies in North America would have broken away from the mother country sooner or later cannot be doubted, but that particular Revolution Of 1776 would have failed within a year, had it not been for Washington. It is not, however, merely the fact that he was a great soldier and statesman which we should remember. The most memorable thing to us, and to all men, is the heroic spirit of the man, which rose in those dreary December days to its greatest height, under conditions so adverse that they had crushed the hope of every one else. Let it be remembered, also, that it was not a spirit of desperation or of ignorance, a reckless daring which did not count the cost. No one knew better than Washington—no one, indeed, so well—the exact state of affairs; for he, conspicuously among great men, always looked facts fearlessly in the face, and never deceived himself. He was under no illusions, and it was this high quality of mind as much as any other which enabled him to win victories.

How he really felt we know from what he wrote to Congress on December 20, when he said:

> It may be thought that I am going a good deal out of the line of my duty to adopt these measures or to advise thus freely.
>
> A character to lose, an estate to forfeit, the inestimable blessing of liberty at stake, and a life devoted, must be my excuse.

These were the thoughts in his mind when he was planning this masterly campaign. These same thoughts, we may readily believe, were with him when his boat was making its way through the ice of the Delaware on Christmas Eve. It was a very solemn moment, and he was the only man in the darkness of that night who fully understood what was at stake; but then, as always, he was calm and serious, with a high courage which nothing could depress.

The familiar picture of a later day depicts Washington crossing the Delaware at the head of his soldiers. He is standing up in the boat, looking forward in the teeth of the storm. It matters little whether the work of the painter is in exact accordance with the real scene or not.

The daring courage, the high resolve, the stern look forward and onward, which the artist strove to show in the great leader, are all vitally true. For we may be sure that the man who led that well-planned but desperate assault, surrounded by darker conditions than the storms of nature which gathered about his boat, and carrying with him the fortunes of his country, was at that moment one of the most heroic figures in history.

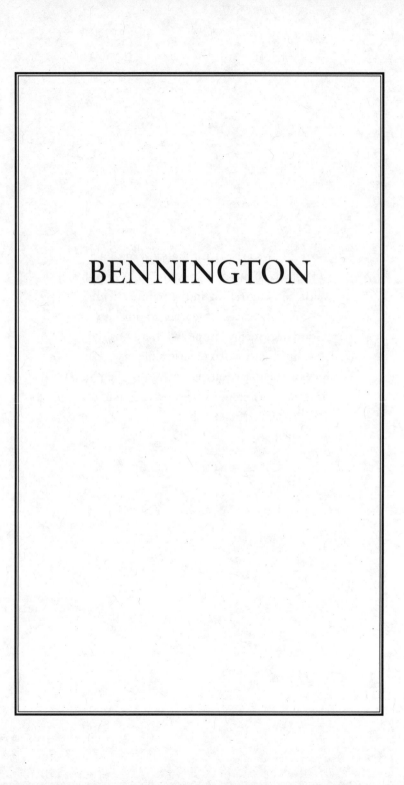

BENNINGTON

We are but warriors for the working-day;
Our gayness and our guilt are all besmirch'd
With rainy marching in the painful field;
There's not a piece of feather in our host
(Good argument, I hope, we shall not fly),
And time hath worn us into slovenry.
But, by the mass, our hearts are in the trim,
And my poor soldiers tell me, yet ere night
They'll be in fresher robes.

—HENRY V.

BENNINGTON

The battle of Saratoga is included by Sir Edward Creasy among his fifteen decisive battles which have, by their result, affected the history of the world. It is true that the American Revolution was saved by Washington in the remarkable Princeton and Trenton campaign, but it is equally true that the surrender of Burgoyne at Saratoga, in the following autumn, turned the scale decisively in favor of the colonists by the impression which it made in Europe. It was the destruction of Burgoyne's army which determined France to aid the Americans against England. Hence came the French alliance, the French troops, and, what was of far more importance, a French fleet by which Washington was finally able to get control of the sea, and in this way cut off Cornwallis at Yorktown and bring the Revolution to a successful close.

That which led, however, more directly than anything else to the final surrender at Saratoga was the fight at Bennington, by which Burgoyne's army was severely crippled and weakened, and by which also, the hardy militia of the North eastern States were led to turn out in large numbers and join the army of Gates.

The English ministry had built great hopes upon Burgoyne's expedition, and neither expense nor effort had been spared to make it successful. He was amply furnished with money and supplies as well as with English and German troops, the latter of whom were bought from their wretched little princes by the payment of generous subsidies. With an admirably equipped army of over seven thousand men, and accompanied by a large force of Indian allies, Burgoyne had started in May, 1777, from Canada. His plan was to make his way by the lakes to the head waters of the Hudson, and thence southward along the river to New York, where he was to unite with Sir William Howe and the main army; in this way cutting the colonies in two, and separating New England from the rest of the country.

At first all went well. The Americans were pushed back from their posts on the lakes, and by the end of July Burgoyne was at the head waters of the Hudson. He had already sent out a force, under St. Leger, to take possession of the valley of the Mohawk—an expedition which finally resulted in the defeat of the British by Herkimer, and the capture of Fort Stanwix. To aid St. Leger by a diversion, and also to capture certain magazines which were reported to be at Bennington, Burgoyne sent another expedition to the eastward. This force consisted of about five hundred and fifty white troops, chiefly Hessians, and one hundred and fifty Indians, all under the command of Colonel Baum. They were within four miles of Bennington on August 13, 1777, and encamped on a hill just within the boundaries of the State of New York. The news of the advance of Burgoyne had already roused the people of New York and New Hampshire, and the legislature of the latter State had ordered General Stark with a brigade of militia to stop the progress of the enemy on the western frontier. Stark raised his standard at Charlestown on the Connecticut River, and the militia poured into his camp. Disregarding Schuyler's orders to join the main American army, which was falling back before Burgoyne, Stark, as soon as he heard of the expedition against Bennington, marched at once to meet Baum. He was within a mile of the British camp on August 14, and vainly endeavored to draw Baum into action. On the 15th it rained heavily, and the British forces occupied the time in intrenching themselves strongly upon the hill which they held. Baum meantime had already sent to Burgoyne for reinforcements, and Burgoyne had detached Colonel Breymann with over six hundred regular troops to go to Baum's assistance. On the 16th the weather cleared, and Stark, who had been reinforced by militia from western Massachusetts, determined to attack.

Early in the day he sent men, under Nichols and Herrick, to get into the rear of Baum's position. The German officer, ignorant of the country and of the nature of the warfare in which he was engaged, noticed small bodies of men in their shirtsleeves, and carrying guns without bayonets, making their way to the rear of his intrenchments. With singular stupidity he concluded that they were Tory inhabitants of the country who were coming to his assistance, and made no attempt to stop them. In this way Stark was enabled to mass about five hundred men in the rear of the enemy's position. Distracting the attention of the British by a feint, Stark also moved about two hundred men to the right, and having thus brought his forces into position he ordered a general assault, and the Americans proceeded to storm the British intrenchments on every side. The fight was a very hot one, and lasted some two hours. The Indians, at the beginning of the action, slipped away between the American detachments, but the British and German regulars stubbornly stood their ground. It is difficult to get at the exact numbers of the American troops, but Stark seems to have had between fifteen hundred and two thousand militia. He thus outnumbered his enemy nearly three to one, but his men were merely country militia, farmers of the New England States, very imperfectly disciplined, and armed only with muskets and fowling-pieces, without bayonets or side-arms. On the other side Baum had the most highly disciplined troops of England and Germany under his command, well armed and equipped, and he was moreover strongly intrenched with artillery well placed behind the breastworks. The advantage in the fight should have been clearly with Baum and his regulars, who merely had to hold an intrenched hill.

It was not a battle in which either military strategy or a scientific management of troops was displayed. All that Stark did was to place his men so that they could attack the enemy's position on every side, and then the Americans went at it, firing as they pressed on. The British and Germans stood their ground stubbornly, while the New England farmers rushed up to within eight yards of the cannon, and picked off the men who manned the guns. Stark himself was in the midst of the fray, fighting with his soldiers, and came out of the conflict so blackened with powder and smoke that he could hardly be recognized. One desperate assault succeeded another, while the firing on both sides was so incessant as to make, in Stark's own words, a "continuous roar." At the end of two hours the Americans finally swarmed over the intrenchments, beating down the soldiers with their clubbed muskets. Baum ordered his infantry with the bayonet and the dragoons with their sabers to force their way through, but the Americans repulsed this final charge, and Baum himself fell mortally wounded. All was then over, and the British forces surrendered.

It was only just in time, for Breymann, who had taken thirty hours to march some twenty-four miles, came up just after Baum's men had laid down their arms. It seemed for a moment as if all that had been gained might be lost. The Americans, attacked by this fresh foe, wavered; but Stark rallied his line, and putting in Warner, with one hundred and fifty Vermont men who had just come on the field, stopped Breymann's advance, and finally forced him to retreat with a loss of nearly one half his men. The Americans lost in killed and wounded some seventy men, and the Germans and British about twice as many, but the Americans took about seven hundred prisoners, and completely wrecked the forces of Baum and Breymann.

The blow was a severe one, and Burgoyne's army never recovered from it. Not only had he lost nearly a thousand of his best troops, besides cannon, arms, and munitions of war, but the defeat affected the spirits of his army and destroyed his hold over his Indian allies, who began to desert in large numbers. Bennington, in fact, was one of the most important fights of the Revolution, contributing as it did so largely to the final surrender of Burgoyne's whole army at Saratoga, and the utter ruin of the British invasion from the North. It is also interesting as an extremely gallant bit of fighting. As has been said, there was no strategy displayed, and there were no military operations of the higher kind. There stood the enemy strongly intrenched on a hill, and Stark, calling his un-disciplined levies about him, went at them. He himself was a man of the highest courage and a reckless fighter. It was Stark who held the railfence at Bunker Hill, and who led the van when Sullivan's division poured into Trenton from the river road. He was admirably adapted for the precise work which was necessary at Bennington, and he and his men fought well their hand-to-hand fight on that hot August day, and carried the intrenchments filled with regular troops and defended by artillery. It was a daring feat of arms, as well as a battle which had an important effect upon the course of history and upon the fate of the British empire in America.

KING'S MOUNTAIN

Our fortress is the good greenwood,
    Our tent the cypress tree;
We know the forest round us
    As seamen know the sea.
We know its walls of thorny vines,
    Its glades of reedy grass,
Its safe and silent islands
    Within the dark morass.

—BRYANT.

KING'S MOUNTAIN

The close of the year 1780 was, in the Southern States, the darkest time of the Revolutionary struggle. Cornwallis had just destroyed the army of Gates at Camden, and his two formidable lieutenants, Tarlton the light horseman, and Ferguson the skilled rifleman, had destroyed or scattered all the smaller bands that had been fighting for the patriot cause. The red dragoons rode hither and thither, and all through Georgia and South Carolina none dared lift their heads to oppose them, while North Carolina lay at the feet of Cornwallis, as he started through it with his army to march into Virginia. There was no organized force against him, and the cause of the patriots seemed hopeless. It was at this hour that the wild backwoodsmen of the western border gathered to strike a blow for liberty.

When Cornwallis invaded North Carolina he sent Ferguson into the western part of the State to crush out any of the patriot forces that might still be lingering among the foot-hills. Ferguson was a very gallant and able officer, and a man of much influence with the people wherever he went, so that he was peculiarly fitted for this scrambling border warfare. He had under him a battalion of regular troops and several other battalions of Tory militia, in all eleven or twelve hundred men.

He shattered and drove the small bands of Whigs that were yet in arms, and finally pushed to the foot of the mountain wall, till he could see in his front the high ranges of the Great Smokies. Here he learned for the first time that beyond the mountains there lay a few hamlets of frontiersmen, whose homes were on what were then called the Western Waters, that is, the waters which flowed into the Mississippi. To these he sent word that if they did not prove loyal to the king, he would cross their mountains, hang their leaders, and burn their villages.

Beyond the, mountains, in the valleys of the Holston and Watauga, dwelt men who were stout of heart and mighty in battle, and when they heard the threats of Ferguson they burned with a sullen flame of anger.

Hitherto the foes against whom they had warred had been not the British, but the Indian allies of the British, Creek, and Cherokee, and Shawnee.

Now that the army of the king had come to their thresholds, they turned to meet it as fiercely as they had met his Indian allies. Among the backwoodsmen of this region there were at that time three men of special note: Sevier, who afterward became governor of Tennessee; Shelby, who afterward became governor of Kentucky; and Campbell, the Virginian, who died in the Revolutionary War. Sevier had given a great barbecue, where oxen and deer were roasted whole, while horseraces were run, and the backwoodsmen tried their skill as marksmen and wrestlers. In the midst of the feasting Shelby appeared, hot with hard riding, to tell of the approach of Ferguson and the British. Immediately the feasting was stopped, and the feasters made ready for war. Sevier and Shelby sent word to Campbell to rouse the men of his own district and come without delay, and they sent messengers to and fro in their own neighborhood to summon the settlers from their log huts on the stump-dotted clearings and the hunters from their smoky cabins in the deep woods.

The meeting-place was at the Sycamore Shoals. On the appointed day the backwoodsmen gathered sixteen hundred strong, each man carrying a long rifle, and mounted on a tough, shaggy horse. They were a wild and fierce people, accustomed to the chase and to warfare with the Indians. Their hunting-shirts of buckskin or homespun were girded in by bead-worked belts, and the trappings of their horses were stained red and yellow.

At the gathering there was a black-frocked Presbyterian preacher, and before they started he addressed the tall riflemen in words of burning zeal, urging them to stand stoutly in the battle, and to smite with the sword of the Lord and of Gideon. Then the army started, the backwoods colonels riding in front. Two or three days later, word was brought to Ferguson that the Back-water men had come over the mountains; that the Indian-fighters of the frontier, leaving unguarded their homes on the Western Waters, had crossed by wooded and precipitous defiles to the help of the beaten men of the plains. Ferguson at once fell back, sending out messengers for help. When he came to King's Mountain, a wooded, hog-back hill on the border line between North and South Carolina, he camped on its top, deeming that there he was safe, for he supposed that before the backwoodsmen could come near enough to attack him help would reach him. But the backwoods leaders felt as keenly as he the need of haste, and choosing out nine hundred picked men, the best warriors of their force, and the best mounted and armed, they made a long forced march to assail Ferguson before help could come to him. All night long they rode the dim forest trails and splashed across the fords of the rushing rivers. All the next day, October 16, they rode, until in mid-afternoon, just as a heavy shower cleared away, they came in sight of King's Mountain. The little armies were about equal in numbers.

Ferguson's regulars were armed with the bayonet, and so were some of his Tory militia, whereas the Americans had not a bayonet among them; but they were picked men, confident in their skill as riflemen, and they were so sure of victory that their aim was not only to defeat the British but to capture their whole force. The backwoods colonels, counseling together as they rode at the head of the column, decided to surround the mountain and assail it on all sides. Accordingly the bands of frontiersmen split one from the other, and soon circled the craggy hill where Ferguson's forces were encamped. They left their horses in the rear and immediately began the battle, swarming forward on foot, their commanders leading the attack.

The march had been so quick and the attack so sudden that Ferguson had barely time to marshal his men before the assault was made. Most of his militia he scattered around the top of the hill to fire down at the Americans as they came up, while with his regulars and with a few picked militia he charged with the bayonet in person, first down one side of the mountain and then down the other. Sevier, Shelby, Campbell, and the other colonels of the frontiersmen, led each his force of riflemen straight toward the summit. Each body in turn when charged by the regulars was forced to give way, for there were no bayonets wherewith to meet the foe; but the backwoodsmen retreated only so long as the charge lasted, and the minute that it stopped they stopped too, and came back ever closer to the ridge and ever with a deadlier fire. Ferguson, blowing a silver whistle as a signal to his men, led these charges, sword in hand, on horseback. At last, just as he was once again rallying his men, the riflemen of Sevier and Shelby crowned the top of the ridge.

The gallant British commander became a fair target for the backwoodsmen, and as for the last time he led his men against them, seven bullets entered his body and he fell dead. With his fall resistance ceased.

The regulars and Tories huddled together in a confused mass, while the exultant Americans rushed forward. A flag of truce was hoisted, and all the British who were not dead surrendered.

The victory was complete, and the backwoodsmen at once started to return to their log hamlets and rough, lonely farms. They could not stay, for they dared not leave their homes at the mercy of the Indians. They had rendered a great service; for Cornwallis, when he heard of the disaster to his trusted lieutenant, abandoned his march northward, and retired to South Carolina. When he again resumed the offensive, he found his path barred by stubborn General Greene and his troops of the Continental line.

THE STORMING
OF
STONY POINT

In their ragged regimentals
Stood the old Continentals,
　　Yielding not,
When the grenadiers were lunging,
And like hail fell the plunging
　　Cannon-shot;
　　When the files
　　Of the isles
From the smoky night encampment bore the banner of
　　the rampant Unicorn,
And grummer, grummer, grummer, rolled the roll of the
　　drummer,
　　Through the morn!

Then with eyes to the front all,
And with guns horizontal,
　　Stood our sires;
And the balls whistled deadly,
And in streams flashing redly
　　Blazed the fires;
　　As the roar
　　On the shore
Swept the strong battle-breakers o'er the green-sodded acres
　　Of the plain;
And louder, louder, louder cracked the black gunpowder,
　　Cracked amain!

　　　　　　　　—GUY HUMPHREY MCMASTER.

THE STORMING OF
STONY POINT

One of the heroic figures of the Revolution was
Anthony Wayne, Major-General of the Continental
line. With the exception of Washington, and perhaps
Greene, he was the best general the Americans developed
in the contest; and without exception he showed himself
to be the hardest fighter produced on either side. He
belongs, as regards this latter characteristic, with the
men like Winfield Scott, Phil Kearney, Hancock, and
Forrest, who reveled in the danger and the actual shock
of arms.

Indeed, his eager love of battle, and splendid disregard
of peril, have made many writers forget his really great
qualities as a general.

Soldiers are always prompt to recognize the prime virtue
of physical courage, and Wayne's followers christened
their daring commander "Mad Anthony," in loving
allusion to his reckless bravery. It is perfectly true that
Wayne had this courage, and that he was a born fighter;
otherwise, he never would have been a great commander.
A man who lacks the fondness for fighting, the eager
desire to punish his adversary, and the willingness to

suffer punishment in return, may be a great organizer, like McClellan, but can never become a great general or win great victories. There are, however, plenty of men who, though they possess these fine manly traits, yet lack the head to command an army; but Wayne had not only the heart and the hand but the head likewise.

No man could dare as greatly as he did without incurring the risk of an occasional check; but he was an able and bold tactician, a vigilant and cautious leader, well fitted to bear the terrible burden of responsibility which rests upon a commander-in-chief.

Of course, at times he had some rather severe lessons. Quite early in his career, just after the battle of the Brandywine, when he was set to watch the enemy, he was surprised at night by the British general Grey, a redoubtable fighter, who attacked him with the bayonet, killed a number of his men, and forced him to fall back some distance from the field of action. This mortifying experience had no effect whatever on Wayne's courage or self-reliance, but it did give him a valuable lesson in caution. He showed what he had learned by the skill with which, many years later, he conducted the famous campaign in which he overthrew the Northwestern Indians at the Fight of the Fallen Timbers.

Wayne's favorite weapon was the bayonet, and, like Scott he taught his troops, until they were able in the shock of hand-to-hand conflict to overthrow the renowned British infantry, who have always justly prided themselves on their prowess with cold steel. At the battle of Germantown it was Wayne's troops who, falling on with the bayonet, drove the Hessians and the British light infantry, and only retreated under orders when the attack had failed elsewhere. At Monmouth it was Wayne and his Continentals who first checked the British advance by repulsing the bayonet charge of the guards and grenadiers.

Washington, a true leader of men, was prompt to recognize in Wayne a soldier to whom could be intrusted any especially difficult enterprise which called for the exercise alike of intelligence and of cool daring.

In the summer of 1780 he was very anxious to capture the British fort at Stony Point, which commanded the Hudson. It was impracticable to attack it by regular siege while the British frigates lay in the river, and the defenses ere so strong that open assault by daylight was equally out of the question. Accordingly Washington suggested to Wayne that he try a night attack. Wayne eagerly caught at the idea. It was exactly the kind of enterprise in which he delighted. The fort was on a rocky promontory, surrounded on three sides by water, and on the fourth by a neck of land, which was for the most part mere morass. It was across this neck of land that any attacking column had to move. The garrison was six hundred strong. To deliver the assault Wayne took nine hundred men. The American army was camped about fourteen miles from Stony Point. One July afternoon Wayne started, and led his troops in single file along the narrow rocky roads, reaching the hills on the mainland near the fort after nightfall. He divided his force into two columns, to advance one along each side of the neck, detaching two companies of North Carolina troops to move in between the two columns and make a false attack.

The rest of the force consisted of New Englanders, Pennsylvanians, and Virginians. Each attacking column was divided into three parts, a forlorn hope of twenty men leading, which was followed by an advance guard of one hundred and twenty, and then by the main body. At the time commanding officers still carried spontoons, and other old-time weapons, and Wayne, who himself led the right column, directed its movements spear in hand. It was nearly midnight when the Americans began to press along the causeways toward the fort. Before they were near the walls they were discovered, and the British opened a heavy fire of great guns and musketry, to which the Carolinians, who were advancing between the two columns, responded in their turn, according to orders; but the men in the columns were forbidden to fire. Wayne had warned them that their work must be done with the bayonet, and their muskets were not even loaded. Moreover, so strict was the discipline that no one was allowed to leave the ranks, and when one of the men did so an officer promptly ran him through the body.

No sooner had the British opened fire than the charging columns broke into a run, and in a moment the forlorn hopes plunged into the abattis of fallen timber which the British had constructed just without the walls. On the left, the forlorn hope was very roughly handled, no less than seventeen of the twenty men being either killed or wounded, but as the columns came up both burst through the down timber and swarmed up the long, sloping embankments of the fort. The British fought well, cheering loudly as their volley's rang, but the Americans would not be denied, and pushed silently on to end the contest with the bayonet. A bullet struck Wayne in the head. He fell, but struggled to his feet and forward, two of his officers supporting him. A rumor went among the men that he was dead, but it only impelled them to charge home, more fiercely than ever.

With a rush the troops swept to the top of the wall. A fierce but short fight followed in the intense darkness, which was lit only by the flashes from the British muskets. The Americans did not fire, trusting solely to the bayonet. The two columns had kept almost equal pace, and they swept into the fort from opposite sides at the same moment. The three men who first got over the walls were all wounded, but one of them hauled down the British flag. The Americans had the advantage which always comes from delivering an attack that is thrust home. Their muskets were unloaded and they could not hesitate; so, running boldly into close quarters, they fought hand to hand with their foes and speedily overthrew them. For a moment the bayonets flashed and played; then the British lines broke as their assailants thronged against them, and the struggle was over. The Americans had lost a hundred in killed and wounded. Of the British sixty-three had been slain and very many wounded, every one of the dead or disabled having suffered from the bayonet. A curious coincidence was that the number of the dead happened to be exactly equal to the number of Wayne's men who had been killed in the night attack by the English general, Grey.

There was great rejoicing among the Americans over the successful issue of the attack. Wayne speedily recovered from his wound, and in the joy of his victory it weighed but slightly. He had performed a most notable feat. No night attack of the kind was ever delivered with greater boldness, skill, and success. When the Revolutionary War broke out the American armies were composed merely of armed yeomen, stalwart men, of good courage, and fairly proficient in the use of their weapons, but entirely without the training which alone could enable them to withstand the attack of the British regulars in the open, or to deliver an attack themselves. Washington's victory at Trenton was the first encounter which showed that the Americans were to be feared when they took the offensive. With the exception of the battle of Trenton, and perhaps of Greene's fight at Eutaw Springs, Wayne's feat was the most successful illustration of daring and victorious attack by an American army that occurred during the war; and, unlike Greene, who was only able to fight a drawn battle, Wayne's triumph was complete. At Monmouth he had shown, as he afterward showed against Cornwallis, that his troops could meet the renowned British regulars on even terms in the open. At Stony Point he showed that he could lead them to a triumphant assault with the bayonet against regulars who held a fortified place of strength. No American commander has ever displayed greater energy and daring, a more resolute courage, or readier resource, than the chief of the hard-fighting Revolutionary generals, Mad Anthony Wayne.

GOUVERNEUR MORRIS

MORRIS

PARIS. AUGUST 10, 1792.

Justum et tenacem propositi virum
Non civium ardor prava jubentium,
   Non vultus instantis tyranni
      Mente quatit solida, neque Auster
Dux inquieti turbidus Hadriae,
Nec fulminantis magna manus Jovis:
   Si fractus illabatur orbis,
      Impavidum ferient ruinae.

—HOR., LIB. III. CARM. III.

GOUVERNEUR MORRIS

The 10th of August, 1792, was one of the most memorable days of the French Revolution. It was the day on which the French monarchy received its death-blow, and was accompanied by fighting and bloodshed which filled Paris with terror. In the morning before daybreak the tocsin had sounded, and not long after the mob of Paris, headed by the Marseillais, "Six hundred men not afraid to die," who had been summoned there by Barbaroux, were marching upon the Tuileries. The king, or rather the queen, had at last determined to make a stand and to defend the throne.

The Swiss Guards were there at the palace, well posted to protect the inner court; and there, too, were the National Guards, who were expected to uphold the government and guard the king. The tide of people poured on through the streets, gathering strength as they went the Marseillais, the armed bands, the Sections, and a vast floating mob. The crowd drew nearer and nearer, but the squadrons of the National Guards, who were to check the advance, did not stir. It is not apparent, indeed, that they made any resistance, and the king and his family at eight o'clock lost heart and deserted the Tuileries, to take refuge with the National Convention. The multitude then passed into the court of the Carrousel, unchecked by the National Guards, and were face to face with the Swiss.

Deserted by their king, the Swiss knew not how to act, but still stood their ground. There was some parleying, and at last the Marseillais fired a cannon. Then the Swiss fired. They were disciplined troops, and their fire was effective. There was a heavy slaughter and the mob recoiled, leaving their cannon, which the Swiss seized. The Revolutionists, however, returned to the charge, and the fight raged on both sides, the Swiss holding their ground firmly.

Suddenly, from the legislative hall, came an order from the king to the Swiss to cease firing. It was their death warrant. Paralyzed by the order, they knew not what to do. The mob poured in, and most of the gallant Swiss were slaughtered where they stood. Others escaped from the Tuileries only to meet their death in the street. The palace was sacked and the raging mob was in possession of the city. No man's life was safe, least of all those who were known to be friends of the king, who were nobles, or who had any connection with the court. Some of these people whose lives were thus in peril at the hands of the bloodstained and furious mob had been the allies of the United States, and had fought under Washington in the war for American independence. In their anguish and distress their thoughts recurred to the country which they had served in its hour of trial, three thousand miles away. They sought the legation of the United States and turned to the American minister for protection.

Such an exercise of humanity at that moment was not a duty that any man craved. In those terrible days in Paris, the representatives of foreign governments were hardly safer than any one else. Many of the ambassadors and ministers had already left the country, and others were even then abandoning their posts, which it seemed impossible to hold at such a time. But the American minister stood his ground. Gouverneur Morris was not a man to shrink from what he knew to be his duty. He had been a leading patriot in our revolution; he had served in the Continental Congress, and with Robert Morris in the difficult work of the Treasury, when all our resources seemed to be at their lowest ebb. In 1788 he had gone abroad on private business, and had been much in Paris, where he had witnessed the beginning of the French Revolution and had been consulted by men on both sides. In 1790, by Washington's direction, he had gone to London and had consulted the ministry there as to whether they would receive an American minister. Thence he had returned to Paris, and at the beginning Of 1792 Washington appointed him minister of the United States to France.

As an American, Morris's sympathies had run strongly in favor of the movement to relieve France from the despotism under which she was sinking, and to give her a better and more liberal government. But, as the Revolution progressed, he became outraged and disgusted by the methods employed. He felt a profound contempt for both sides. The inability of those who were conducting the Revolution to carry out intelligent plans or maintain order, and the feebleness of the king and his advisers, were alike odious to the man with American conceptions of ordered liberty. He was especially revolted by the bloodshed and cruelty, constantly gathering in strength, which were displayed by the revolutionists, and he had gone to the very verge of diplomatic propriety in advising the ministers of the king in regard to the policies to be pursued, and, as he foresaw what was coming, in urging the king himself to leave France. All his efforts and all his advice, like those of other intelligent men who kept their heads during the whirl of the Revolution, were alike vain.

On August 10 the gathering storm broke with full force, and the populace rose in arms to sweep away the tottering throne. Then it was that these people, fleeing for their lives, came to the representative of the country for which many of them had fought, and on both public and private grounds besought the protection of the American minister. Let me tell what happened in the words of an eye-witness, an American gentleman who was in Paris at that time, and who published the following account of his experiences:

On the ever memorable 10th of August, after viewing the destruction of the Royal Swiss Guards and the dispersion of the Paris militia by a band of foreign and native incendiaries, the writer thought it his duty to visit the Minister, who had not been out of his hotel since the insurrection began, and, as was to be expected, would be anxious to learn what was passing without doors. He was surrounded by the old Count d'Estaing, and about a dozen other persons of distinction, of different sexes, who had, from their connection with the United States, been his most intimate acquaintances at Paris, and who had taken refuge with him for protection from the bloodhounds which, in the forms of men and women, were prowling in the streets at the time. All was silence here, except that silence was occasionally interrupted by the crying of the women and children. As I retired, the Minister took me aside, and observed: "I have no doubt, sir, but there are persons on the watch who would find fault with my conduct as Minister in receiving and protecting these people, but I call on you to witness the declaration which I now make, and that is that they were not invited to my house, but came of their own accord. Whether my house will be a protection to them or to me, God only knows, but I will not turn them out of it, let what will happen to me," to which he added, "you see, sir, they are all persons to whom our country is more or less indebted, and it would be inhuman to force them into the hands of the assassins, had they no such claim upon me."

Nothing can be added to this simple account, and no American can read it or repeat the words of Mr. Morris without feeling even now, a hundred years after the event, a glow of pride that such words were uttered at such a time by the man who represented the United States.

After August 10, when matters in Paris became still worse, Mr. Morris still stayed at his post. Let me give, in his own words, what he did and his reasons for it:

> The different ambassadors and ministers are all taking their flight, and if I stay I shall be alone. I mean, however, to stay, unless circumstances should command me away, because, in the admitted case that my letters of credence are to the monarchy, and not to the Republic of France, it becomes a matter of indifference whether I remain in this country or go to England during the time which may be needful to obtain your orders, or to produce a settlement of affairs here. Going hence, however, would look like taking part against the late Revolution, and I am not only unauthorized in this respect, but I am bound to suppose that if the great majority of the nation adhere to the new form, the United States will approve thereof; because, in the first place, we have no right to prescribe to this country the government they shall adopt, and next, because the basis of our own Constitution is the indefeasible right of the people to establish it.

> Among those who are leaving Paris is the Venetian ambassador. He was furnished with passports from the Office of Foreign Affairs, but he was, neverthe-

less, stopped at the barrier, was conducted to the Hotel de Ville, was there questioned for hours, and his carriages examined and searched. This violation of the rights of ambassadors could not fail, as you may suppose, to make an impression. It has been broadly hinted to me that the honor of my country and my own require that I should go away.

But I am of a different opinion, and rather think that those who give such hints are somewhat influenced by fear. It is true that the position is not without danger, but I presume that when the President did me the honor of naming me to this embassy, it was not for my personal pleasure or safety, but to promote the interests of my country. These, therefore, I shall continue to pursue to the best of my judgment, and as to consequences, they are in the hand of God.

He remained there until his successor arrived. When all others fled, he was faithful, and such conduct should never be forgotten. Mr. Morris not only risked his life, but he took a heavy responsibility, and laid himself open to severe attack for having protected defenseless people against the assaults of the mob. But his courageous humanity is something which should ever be remembered, and ought always to be characteristic of the men who represent the United States in foreign countries. When we recall the French Revolution, it is cheering to think of that fearless figure of the American minister, standing firm and calm in the midst of those awful scenes, with sacked palaces, slaughtered soldiers, and a bloodstained mob about him, regardless of danger to himself, determined to do his duty to his country, and to those to whom his country was indebted.

THE BURNING
OF THE
"PHILADELPHIA"

And say besides, that in Aleppo once,
Where a malignant and a turban'd Turk
Beat a Venetian and traduced the state,
I took by the throat the circumcised dog
And smote him, thus.

—OTHELLO.

THE BURNING OF THE "PHILADELPHIA"

It is difficult to conceive that there ever was a time when the United States paid a money tribute to anybody. It is even more difficult to imagine the United States paying blackmail to a set of small piratical tribes on the coast of Africa. Yet this is precisely what we once did with the Barbary powers, as they were called the States of Morocco, Tunis, Tripoli, and Algiers, lying along the northern coast of Africa.

The only excuse to be made for such action was that we merely followed the example of Christendom. The civilized people of the world were then in the habit of paying sums of money to these miserable pirates, in order to secure immunity for their merchant vessels in the Mediterranean. For this purpose Congress appropriated money, and treaties were made by the President and ratified by the Senate. On one occasion, at least, Congress actually revoked the authorization of some new ships for the navy, and appropriated more money than was required to build the men-of-war in order to buy off the Barbary powers. The fund for this disgraceful purpose was known as the "Mediterranean fund," and was intrusted to the Secretary of State to be disbursed by him in his discretion. After we had our brush with France, however, in 1798, and after Truxtun's brilliant victory over the French frigate L'Insurgente in the following year, it occurred to our government that perhaps there was a more direct as well as a more manly way of dealing with the Barbary pirates than by feebly paying them tribute, and in 1801 a small squadron, under Commodore Dale, proceeded to the Mediterranean.

At the same time events occurred which showed strikingly the absurdity as well as the weakness of this policy of paying blackmail to pirates.

The Bashaw of Tripoli, complaining that we had given more money to some of the Algerian ministers than we had to him, and also that we had presented Algiers with a frigate, declared war upon us, and cut down the flag-staff in front of the residence of the American consul. At the same time, and for the same reason, Morocco and Tunis began to grumble at the treatment which they had received. The fact was that, with nations as with individuals, when the payment of blackmail is once begun there is no end to it. The appearance, however, of our little squadron in the Mediterranean showed at once the superiority of a policy of force over one of cowardly submission. Morocco and Tunis immediately stopped their grumbling and came to terms with the United States, and this left us free to deal with Tripoli.

Commodore Dale had sailed before the declaration of war by Tripoli was known, and he was therefore hampered by his orders, which permitted him only to protect our commerce, and which forbade actual hostilities.

Nevertheless, even under these limited orders, the Enterprise, of twelve guns, commanded by Lieutenant Sterrett, fought an action with the Tripolitan ship Tripoli, of fourteen guns. The engagement lasted three hours, when the Tripoli struck, having lost her mizzenmast, and with twenty of her crew killed and thirty wounded. Sterrett, having no orders to make captures, threw all the guns and ammunition of the Tripoli overboard, cut away her remaining masts, and left her with only one spar and a single sail to drift back to Tripoli, as a hint to the Bashaw of the new American policy.

In 1803 the command of our fleet in the Mediterranean was taken by Commodore Preble, who had just succeeded in forcing satisfaction from Morocco for an attack made upon our merchantmen by a vessel from Tangier. He also proclaimed a blockade of Tripoli and was preparing to enforce it when the news reached him that the frigate Philadelphia, forty-four guns, commanded by Captain Bainbridge, and one of the best ships in our navy, had gone upon a reef in the harbor of Tripoli, while pursuing a vessel there, and had been surrounded and captured, with all her crew, by the Tripolitan gunboats, when she was entirely helpless either to fight or sail. This was a very serious blow to our navy and to our operations against Tripoli. It not only weakened our forces, but it was also a great help to the enemy. The Tripolitans got the Philadelphia off the rocks, towed her into the harbor, and anchored her close under the guns of their forts. They also replaced her batteries, and prepared to make her ready for sea, where she would have been a most formidable danger to our shipping.

Under these circumstances Stephen Decatur, a young lieutenant in command of the Enterprise, offered to Commodore Preble to go into the harbor and destroy the Philadelphia. Some delay ensued, as our squadron was driven by severe gales from the Tripolitan coast; but at last, in January, 1804, Preble gave orders to Decatur to undertake the work for which he had volunteered. A small vessel known as a ketch had been recently captured from the Tripolitans by Decatur, and this prize was now named the Intrepid, and assigned to him for the work he had in hand. He took seventy men from his own ship, the Enterprise, and put them on the Intrepid, and then, accompanied by Lieutenant Stewart in the Siren, who was to support him, he set sail for Tripoli. He and his crew were very much cramped as well as badly fed on the little vessel which had been given to them, but they succeeded, nevertheless, in reaching Tripoli in safety, accompanied by the Siren.

For nearly a week they were unable to approach the harbor, owing to severe gales which threatened the loss of their vessel; but on February 16 the weather moderated and Decatur determined to go in. It is well to recall, briefly, the extreme peril of the attack which he was about to make. The Philadelphia, with forty guns mounted, double-shotted, and ready for firing, and manned by a full complement of men, was moored within half a gunshot of the Bashaw's castle, the mole and crown batteries, and within range of ten other batteries, mounting, altogether, one hundred and fifteen guns. Some Tripolitan cruisers, two galleys, and nineteen gunboats also lay between the Philadelphia and the shore. Into the midst of this powerful armament Decatur had to go with his little vessel of sixty tons, carrying four small guns and having a crew of seventy-five men.

The Americans, however, were entirely undismayed by the odds against them, and at seven o'clock Decatur went into the harbor between the reef and shoal which formed its mouth. He steered on steadily toward the Philadelphia, the breeze getting constantly lighter, and by half-past nine was within two hundred yards of the frigate. As they approached Decatur stood at the helm with the pilot, only two or three men showing on deck and the rest of the crew lying hidden under the bulwarks. In this way he drifted to within nearly twenty yards of the Philadelphia.

The suspicions of the Tripolitans, however, were not aroused, and when they hailed the Intrepid, the pilot answered that they had lost their anchors in a gale, and asked that they might run a warp to the frigate and ride by her. While the talk went on the Intrepid's boat shoved off with the rope, and pulling to the fore-chains of the Philadelphia, made the line fast. A few of the crew then began to haul on the lines, and thus the Intrepid was drawn gradually toward the frigate.

The suspicions of the Tripolitans were now at last awakened. They raised the cry of "Americanos!" and ordered off the Intrepid, but it was too late. As the vessels came in contact, Decatur sprang up the main chains of the Philadelphia, calling out the order to board. He was rapidly followed by his officers and men, and as they swarmed over the rails and came upon the deck, the Tripolitan crew gathered, panic-stricken, in a confused mass on the forecastle. Decatur waited a moment until his men were behind him, and then, placing himself at their head, drew his sword and rushed upon the Tripolitans. There was a very short struggle, and the Tripolitans, crowded together, terrified and surprised, were cut down or driven overboard. In five minutes the ship was cleared of the enemy.

Decatur would have liked to have taken the Philadelphia out of the harbor, but that was impossible. He therefore gave orders to burn the ship, and his men, who had been thoroughly instructed in what they were to do, dispersed into all parts of the frigate with the combustibles which had been prepared, and in a few minutes, so well and quickly was the work done, the flames broke out in all parts of the Philadelphia. As soon as this was effected the order was given to return to the Intrepid.

Without confusion the men obeyed. It was a moment of great danger, for fire was breaking out on all sides, and the Intrepid herself, filled as she was with powder and combustibles, was in great peril of sudden destruction. The rapidity of Decatur's movements, however, saved everything. The cables were cut, the sweeps got out, and the Intrepid drew rapidly away from the burning frigate. It was a magnificent sight as the flames burst out over the Philadephia and ran rapidly and fiercely up the masts and rigging. As her guns became heated they were discharged, one battery pouring its shots into the town. Finally the cables parted, and then the Philadelphia, a mass of flames, drifted across the harbor, and blew up. Meantime the batteries of the shipping and the castle had been turned upon the Intrepid, but although the shot struck all around her, she escaped successfully with only one shot through her mainsail, and, joining the Siren, bore away.

This successful attack was carried through by the cool courage of Decatur and the admirable discipline of his men. The hazard was very great, the odds were very heavy, and everything depended on the nerve with which the attack was made and the completeness of the surprise.

Nothing miscarried, and no success could have been more complete.

Nelson, at that time in the Mediterranean, and the best judge of a naval exploit as well as the greatest naval commander who has ever lived, pronounced it "the most bold and daring act of the age." We meet no single feat exactly like it in our own naval history, brilliant as that has been, until we come to Cushing's destruction of the Albemarle in the war of the rebellion. In the years that have elapsed, and among the great events that have occurred since that time, Decatur's burning of the Philadephia has been well-nigh forgotten; but it is one of those feats of arms which illustrate the high courage of American seamen, and which ought always to be remembered.

THE CRUISE
OF THE "WASP"

A crash as when some swollen cloud
  Cracks o'er the tangled trees!
With side to side, and spar to spar,
  Whose smoking decks are these?
I know St. George's blood-red cross,
  Thou mistress of the seas,
But what is she whose streaming bars
  Roll out before the breeze?

Ah, well her iron ribs are knit,
  Whose thunders strive to quell
The bellowing throats, the blazing lips,
  That pealed the Armada's knell!
The mist was cleared,—a wreath of stars
  Rose o'er the crimsoned swell,
And, wavering from its haughty peak,
  The cross of England fell!

—HOLMES.

THE CRUISE OF THE "WASP"

In the war of 1812 the little American navy, including only a dozen frigates and sloops of war, won a series of victories against the English, the hitherto undoubted masters of the sea, that attracted an attention altogether out of proportion to the force of the combatants or the actual damage done. For one hundred and fifty years the English ships of war had failed to find fit rivals in those of any other European power, although they had been matched against each in turn; and when the unknown navy of the new nation growing up across the Atlantic did what no European navy had ever been able to do, not only the English and Americans, but the people of Continental Europe as well, regarded the feat as important out of all proportion to the material aspects of the case. The Americans first proved that the English could be beaten at their own game on the sea. They did what the huge fleets of France, Spain, and Holland had failed to do, and the great modern writers on naval warfare in Continental Europe—men like Jurien de la Graviere—have paid the same attention to these contests of frigates and sloops that they give to whole fleet actions of other wars.

Among the famous ships of the Americans in this war were two named the Wasp. The first was an eighteen-gun

ship-sloop, which at the very outset of the war captured
a British brig-sloop of twenty guns, after an engagement
in which the British fought with great gallantry, but
were knocked to Pieces, while the Americans escaped
comparatively unscathed.

Immediately afterward a British seventy-four captured
the victor. In memory of her the Americans gave the
same name to one of the new sloops they were building.
These sloops were stoutly made, speedy vessels which
in strength and swiftness compared favorably with
any ships of their class in any other navy of the day,
for the American shipwrights were already as famous
as the American gunners and seamen. The new Wasp,
like her sister ships, carried twenty-two guns and a crew
of one hundred and seventy men, and was ship-rigged.
Twenty of her guns were 32-pound carronades, while
for bow-chasers she had two "long Toms." It was in the
year 1814 that the Wasp sailed from the United States
to prey on the navy and commerce of Great Britain.
Her commander was a gallant South Carolinian named
Captain Johnson Blakeley. Her crew were nearly all
native Americans, and were an exceptionally fine set of
men. Instead of staying near the American coasts or of
sailing the high seas, the Wasp at once headed boldly for
the English Channel, to carry the war to the very doors
of the enemy.

At that time the English fleets had destroyed the navies
of every other power of Europe, and had obtained such
complete supremacy over the French that the French

fleets were kept in port. Off these ports lay the great squadrons of the English ships of the line, never, in gale or in calm, relaxing their watch upon the rival war-ships of the French emperor. So close was the blockade of the French ports, and so hopeless were the French of making headway in battle with their antagonists, that not only the great French three-deckers and two-deckers, but their frigates and sloops as well, lay harmless in their harbors, and the English ships patroled the seas unchecked in every direction. A few French privateers still slipped out now and then, and the far bolder and more formidable American privateersmen drove hither and thither across the ocean in their swift schooners and brigantines, and harried the English commerce without mercy.

The Wasp proceeded at once to cruise in the English Channel and off the coasts of England, France, and Spain. Here the water was traversed continually by English fleets and squadrons and single ships of war, which were sometimes convoying detachments of troops for Wellington's Peninsular army, sometimes guarding fleets of merchant vessels bound homeward, and sometimes merely cruising for foes. It was this spot, right in the teeth of the British naval power, that the Wasp chose for her cruising ground. Hither and thither she sailed through the narrow seas, capturing and destroying the merchantmen, and by the seamanship of her crew and the skill and vigilance of her commander, escaping the pursuit of frigate and ship of the line. Before she had been long on the ground, one June morning, while in chase of a couple of merchant ships, she spied a sloop of war, the British brig Reindeer, of eighteen guns and a hundred and twenty men. The Reindeer was a weaker ship than the Wasp, her guns were lighter, and her men fewer; but her commander, Captain Manners, was one of the most gallant men in the splendid British navy, and he promptly took up the gage of battle which the Wasp threw down.

The day was calm and nearly still; only a light wind stirred across the sea. At one o'clock the Wasp's drum beat to quarters, and the sailors and marines gathered at their appointed posts. The drum of the Reindeer responded to the challenge, and with her sails reduced to fighting trim, her guns run out, and every man ready, she came down upon the Yankee ship. On her forecastle she had rigged a light carronade, and coming up from behind, she five times discharged this pointblank into the American sloop; then in the light air the latter luffed round, firing her guns as they bore, and the two ships engaged yard-arm to yard-arm. The guns leaped and thundered as the grimy gunners hurled them out to fire and back again to load, working like demons. For a few minutes the cannonade was tremendous, and the men in the tops could hardly see the decks for the wreck of flying splinters. Then the vessels ground together, and through the open ports the rival gunners hewed, hacked, and thrust at one another, while the black smoke curled up from between the hulls. The English were suffering terribly. Captain Manners himself was wounded, and realizing that he was doomed to defeat unless by some desperate effort he could avert it, he gave the signal to board. At the call the boarders gathered, naked to the waist, black with powder and spattered with blood, cutlass and pistol in hand. But the Americans were ready.

Their marines were drawn up on deck, the pikemen stood behind the bulwarks, and the officers watched, cool and alert, every movement of the foe. Then the British sea-dogs tumbled aboard, only to perish by shot or steel. The combatants slashed and stabbed with savage fury, and the assailants were driven back. Manners sprang to their head to lead them again himself, when a ball fired by one of the sailors in the American tops crashed through his skull, and he fell, sword in hand, with his face to the foe, dying as honorable a death as ever a brave man died in fighting against odds for the flag of his country. As he fell the American officers passed the word to board. With wild cheers the fighting sailormen sprang forward, sweeping the wreck of the British force before them, and in a minute the Reindeer was in their possession.

All of her officers, and nearly two thirds of the crew, were killed or wounded; but they had proved themselves as skillful as they were brave, and twenty-six of the Americans had been killed or wounded.

The Wasp set fire to her prize, and after retiring to a French port to refit, came out again to cruise. For some time she met no antagonist of her own size with which to wage war, and she had to exercise the sharpest vigilance to escape capture. Late one September afternoon, when she could see ships of war all around her, she selected one which was isolated from the others, and decided to run alongside her and try to sink her after nightfall. Accordingly she set her sails in pursuit, and drew steadily toward her antagonist, a big eighteen-gun brig, the Avon, a ship more powerful than the Reindeer. The Avon kept signaling to two other British war vessels which were in sight—one an eighteen-gun brig and the other a twenty-gun ship; they were so close that the Wasp was afraid they would interfere before the combat could be ended.

Nevertheless, Blakeley persevered, and made his attack with equal skill and daring. It was after dark when he ran alongside his opponent, and they began forthwith to exchange furious broadsides. As the ships plunged and wallowed in the seas, the Americans could see the clusters of topmen in the rigging of their opponent, but they knew nothing of the vessel's name or of her force, save only so far as they felt it. The firing was fast and furious, but the British shot with bad aim, while the skilled American gunners hulled their opponent at almost every discharge. In a very few minutes the Avon was in a sinking condition, and she struck her flag and cried for quarter, having lost forty or fifty men, while but three of the Americans had fallen. Before the Wasp could take possession of her opponent, however, the two war vessels to which the Avon had been signaling came up. One of them fired at the Wasp, and as the latter could not fight two new foes, she ran off easily before the wind. Neither of her new antagonists followed her, devoting themselves to picking up the crew of the sinking Avon.

It would be hard to find a braver feat more skillfully performed than this; for Captain Blakeley, with hostile foes all round him, had closed with and sunk one antagonist not greatly his inferior in force, suffering hardly any loss himself, while two of her friends were coming to her help.

Both before and after this the Wasp cruised hither and thither making prizes. Once she came across a convoy of ships bearing arms and munitions to Wellington's army, under the care of a great two-decker.

Hovering about, the swift sloop evaded the two-decker's movements, and actually cut out and captured one of the transports she was guarding, making her escape unharmed. Then she sailed for the high seas. She made several other prizes, and on October 9 spoke a Swedish brig.

This was the last that was ever heard of the gallant Wasp. She never again appeared, and no trace of any of those aboard her was ever found.

Whether she was wrecked on some desert coast, whether she foundered in some furious gale, or what befell her none ever knew. All that is certain is that she perished, and that all on board her met death in some one of the myriad forms in which it must always be faced by those who go down to the sea in ships; and when she sank there sank one of the most gallant ships of the American navy, with as brave a captain and crew as ever sailed from any port of the New World.

THE
"GENERAL
ARMSTRONG"
PRIVATEER

We have fought such a fight for a day and a night
As may never be fought again!
We have won great glory, my men!
And a day less or more
At sea or ashore,
We die—does it matter when?

—TENNYSON.

THE "GENERAL ARMSTRONG" PRIVATEER

In the revolution, and again in the war of 1812, the seas were covered by swift-sailing American privateers, which preyed on the British trade. The hardy seamen of the New England coast, and of New York, Philadelphia, and Baltimore, turned readily from their adventurous careers in the whalers that followed the giants of the ocean in every sea and every clime, and from trading voyages to the uttermost parts of the earth, to go into the business of privateering, which was more remunerative, and not so very much more dangerous, than their ordinary pursuits. By the end of the war of 1812, in particular, the American privateers had won for themselves a formidable position on the ocean.

The schooners, brigs, and brigantines in which the privateersmen sailed were beautifully modeled, and were among the fastest craft afloat. They were usually armed with one heavy gun, the "long Tom," as it was called, arranged on a pivot forward or amidships, and with a few lighter pieces of cannon. They carried strong crews of well-armed men, and their commanders were veteran seamen, used to brave every danger from the elements or from man. So boldly did they prey on the British commerce, that they infested even the Irish Sea and the British Channel, and increased many times the rate of insurance on vessels passing across those waters. They also often did battle with the regular men-of-war of the British, being favorite objects for attack by cutting-out parties from the British frigates and ships of the line, and also frequently encountering in fight the smaller sloops-of-war. Usually, in these contests, the privateers-men were worsted, for they had not the training which is obtained only in a regular service, and they were in no way to be compared to the little fleet of regular vessels which in this same war so gloriously upheld the honor of the American flag. Nevertheless, here and there a privateer commanded by an exceptionally brave and able captain, and manned by an unusually well-trained crew, performed some feat of arms which deserves to rank with anything ever performed by the regular navy. Such a feat was the defense of the brig General Armstrong, in the Portuguese port of Fayal, of the Azores, against an overwhelming British force.

The General Armstrong hailed from New York, and her captain was named Reid. She had a crew of ninety men, and was armed with one heavy 32 pounder and six lighter guns. In December, 1814, she was lying in Fayal, a neutral port, when four British war-vessels, a ship of the line, a frigate and two brigs, hove into sight, and anchored off the mouth of the harbor. The port was neutral, but Portugal was friendly to England, and Reid knew well that the British would pay no respect to the neutrality laws if they thought that at the cost of their violation they could destroy the privateer. He immediately made every preparation to resist an attack. The privateer was anchored close to the shore. The boarding-nettings were got ready, and were stretched to booms thrust outward from the brig's side, so as to check the boarders as they tried to climb over the bulwarks. The guns were loaded and cast loose, and the men went to quarters armed with muskets, boarding-pikes, and cutlasses.

On their side the British made ready to carry the privateer by boarding. The shoals rendered it impossible for the heavy ships to approach, and the lack of wind and the baffling currents also interfered for the moment with the movements of the sloops-of-war. Accordingly recourse was had to a cutting-out party, always a favorite device with the British seamen of that age, who were accustomed to carry French frigates by boarding, and to capture in their boats the heavy privateers and armed merchantmen, as well as the lighter war-vessels of France and Spain.

The British first attempted to get possession of the brig by surprise, sending out but four boats. These worked down near to the brig, under pretense of sounding, trying to get close enough to make a rush and board her. The privateersmen were on their guard, and warned the boats off, and after the warning had been repeated once or twice unheeded, they fired into them, killing and wounding several men. Upon this the boats promptly returned to the ships.

This first check greatly irritated the British captains, and they decided to repeat the experiment that night with a force which would render resistance vain. Accordingly, after it became dark, a dozen boats were sent from the liner and the frigate, manned by four hundred stalwart British seamen, and commanded by the captain of one of the brigs of war. Through the night they rowed straight toward the little privateer lying dark and motionless in the gloom. As before, the privateersmen were ready for their foe, and when they came within range opened fire upon them, first with the long gun and then with the lighter cannon; but the British rowed on with steady strokes, for they were seamen accustomed to victory over every European foe, and danger had no terrors for them. With fierce hurrahs they dashed through the shot-riven smoke and grappled the brig; and the boarders rose, cutlass in hand, ready to spring over the bulwarks. A terrible struggle followed. The British hacked at the boarding-nets and strove to force their way through to the decks of the privateer, while the Americans stabbed the assailants with their long pikes and slashed at them with their cutlasses. The darkness was lit by the flashes of flame from the muskets and the cannon, and the air was rent by the oaths and shouts of the combatants, the heavy trampling on the decks, the groans of the wounded, the din of weapon meeting weapon, and all the savage tumult of a hand-to-hand fight. At the bow the British burst through the boarding-netting, and forced their way to the deck, killing or wounding all three of the lieutenants of the privateer; but when this had happened the boats had elsewhere been beaten back, and Reid, rallying his grim sea-dogs, led them forward with a rush, and the boarding party were all killed or tumbled into the sea. This put an end to the fight.

In some of the boats none but killed and wounded men were left. The others drew slowly off, like crippled wild-fowl, and disappeared in the darkness toward the British squadron. Half of the attacking force had been killed or wounded, while of the Americans but nine had fallen.

The British commodore and all his officers were maddened with anger and shame over the repulse, and were bent upon destroying the privateer at all costs. Next day, after much exertion, one of the war-brigs was warped into position to attack the American, but she first took her station at long range, so that her carronades were not as effective as the pivot gun of the privateer; and so well was the latter handled, that the British brig was repeatedly hulled, and finally was actually driven off. A second attempt was made, however, and this time the sloop-of-war got so close that she could use her heavy carronades, which put the privateer completely at her mercy. Then Captain Reid abandoned his brig and sank her, first carrying ashore the guns, and marched inland with his men. They were not further molested; and, if they had lost their brig, they had at least made their foes pay dear for her destruction, for the British had lost twice as many men as there were in the whole hard-fighting crew of the American privateer.

THE BATTLE OF
NEW ORLEANS

The heavy fog of morning
  Still hid the plain from sight,
When came a thread of scarlet
  Marked faintly in the white.
We fired a single cannon,
  And as its thunders rolled,
The mist before us lifted
  In many a heavy fold.
The mist before us lifted,
  And in their bravery fine
Came rushing to their ruin
  The fearless British line.

—THOMAS DUNN ENGLISH.

THE BATTLE OF NEW ORLEANS

When, in 1814, Napoleon was overthrown and forced to retire to Elba, the British troops that had followed Wellington into southern France were left free for use against the Americans. A great expedition was organized to attack and capture New Orleans, and at its head was placed General Pakenham, the brilliant commander of the column that delivered the fatal blow at Salamanca. In December a fleet of British war-ships and transports, carrying thousands of victorious veterans from the Peninsula, and manned by sailors who had grown old in a quarter of a century's triumphant ocean warfare, anchored off the broad lagoons of the Mississippi delta. The few American gunboats were carried after a desperate hand-to-hand struggle, the troops were landed, and on December 23 the advance-guard of two thousand men reached the banks of the Mississippi, but ten miles below New Orleans, and there camped for the night. It seemed as if nothing could save the Creole City from foes who had shown, in the storming of many a Spanish walled town, that they were as ruthless in victory as they were terrible in battle. There were no forts to protect the place, and the militia were ill armed and ill trained. But the hour found the man. On the afternoon of the very day when the British reached the banks of the river the vanguard of Andrew Jackson's Tennesseeans marched into New Orleans. Clad in hunting-shirts of buckskin or homespun, wearing wolfskin and coonskin caps, and carrying their long rifles on their shoulders, the wild soldiery of the backwoods tramped into the little French town. They were tall men, with sinewy frames and piercing eyes. Under "Old Hickory's" lead they had won the bloody battle of the Horseshoe Bend against the Creeks; they had driven the Spaniards from Pensacola; and now they were eager to pit themselves against the most renowned troops of all Europe.

Jackson acted with his usual fiery, hasty decision. It was absolutely necessary to get time in which to throw up some kind of breastworks or defenses for the city, and he at once resolved on a night attack against the British. As for the British, they had no thought of being molested.

They did not dream of an assault from inferior numbers of undisciplined and ill-armed militia, who did not possess so much as bayonets to their guns. They kindled fires along the levees, ate their supper, and then, as the evening fell, noticed a big schooner drop down the river in ghostly silence and bring up opposite to them. The soldiers flocked to the shore, challenging the stranger, and finally fired one or two shots at her. Then suddenly a rough voice was heard, "Now give it to them, for the honor of America!" and a shower of shell and grape fell on the British, driving them off the levee. The stranger was an American man-of-war schooner. The British brought up artillery to drive her off, but before they succeeded Jackson's land troops burst upon them, and a fierce, indecisive struggle followed. In the night all order was speedily lost, and the two sides fought singly or in groups in the utmost confusion. Finally a fog came up and the combatants separated. Jackson drew off four or five miles and camped.

The British had been so roughly handled that they were unable to advance for three or four days, until the entire army came up. When they did advance, it was only to find that Jackson had made good use of the time he had gained by his daring assault. He had thrown up breastworks of mud and logs from the swamp to the river. At first the British tried to batter down these breastworks with their cannon, for they had many more guns than the Americans. A terrible artillery duel followed. For an hour or two the result seemed in doubt; but the American gunners showed themselves to be far more skillful than their antagonists, and gradually getting the upper hand, they finally silenced every piece of British artillery. The Americans had used cotton bales in the embrasures, and the British hogsheads of sugar; but neither worked well, for the cotton caught fire and the sugar hogsheads were ripped and splintered by the roundshot, so that both were abandoned. By the use of red-hot shot the British succeeded in setting on fire the American schooner which had caused them such annoyance on the evening of the night attack; but she had served her purpose, and her destruction caused little anxiety to Jackson.

Having failed in his effort to batter down the American breastworks, and the British artillery having been fairly worsted by the American, Pakenham decided to try open assault. He had ten thousand regular troops, while Jackson had under him but little over five thousand men, who were trained only as he had himself trained them in his Indian campaigns. Not a fourth of them carried bayonets. Both Pakenham and the troops under him were fresh from victories won over the most renowned marshals of Napoleon, and over soldiers that had proved themselves on a hundred stricken fields the masters of all others in Continental Europe.

At Toulouse they had driven Marshal Soult from a position infinitely stronger than that held by Jackson, and yet Soult had under him a veteran army. At Badajoz, Ciudad Rodrigo, and San Sebastian they had carried by open assault fortified towns whose strength made the intrenchments of the Americans seem like the mud walls built by children, though these towns were held by the best soldiers of France.

With such troops to follow him, and with such victories behind him in the past, it did not seem possible to Pakenham that the assault of the terrible British infantry could be successfully met by rough backwoods riflemen fighting under a general as wild and untrained as themselves.

He decreed that the assault should take place on the morning of the eighth. Throughout the previous night the American officers were on the alert, for they could hear the rumbling of artillery in the British camp, the muffled tread of the battalions as they were marched to their points in the line, and all the smothered din of the preparation for assault. Long before dawn the riflemen were awake and drawn up behind the mud walls, where they lolled at ease, or, leaning on their long rifles, peered out through the fog toward the camp of their foes. At last the sun rose and the fog lifted, showing the scarlet array of the splendid British infantry. As soon as the air was clear Pakenham gave the word, and the heavy columns of redcoated grenadiers and kilted Highlanders moved steadily forward. From the American breastworks the great guns opened, but not a rifle cracked. Three fourths of the distance were covered, and the eager soldiers broke into a run; then sheets of flame burst from the breastworks in their front as the wild riflemen of the backwoods rose and fired, line upon line. Under the sweeping hail the head of the British advance was shattered, and the whole column stopped. Then it surged forward again, almost to the foot of the breastworks; but not a man lived to reach them, and in a moment more the troops broke and ran back. Mad with shame and rage, Pakenham rode among them to rally and lead them forward, and the officers sprang around him, smiting the fugitives with their swords and cheering on the men who stood. For a moment the troops halted, and again came forward to the charge; but again they were met by a hail of bullets from the backwoods rifles. One shot struck Pakenham himself. He reeled and fell from the saddle, and was carried off the field. The second and third in command fell also, and then all attempts at further advance were abandoned, and the British troops ran back to their lines. Another assault had meanwhile been made by a column close to the river, the charging soldiers rushing to the top of the breastworks; but they were all killed or driven back. A body of troops had also been sent across the river, where they routed a small detachment of Kentucky militia; but they were, of course, recalled when the main assault failed.

At last the men who had conquered the conquerors of Europe had themselves met defeat. Andrew Jackson and his rough riflemen had worsted, in fair fight, a far larger force of the best of Wellington's veterans, and had accomplished what no French marshal and no French troops had been able to accomplish throughout the long war in the Spanish peninsula. For a week the sullen British lay in their lines; then, abandoning their heavy artillery, they marched back to the ships and sailed for Europe.

JOHN QUINCY ADAMS AND THE RIGHT OF PETITION

He rests with the immortals; his journey has been long:
For him no wail of sorrow, but a paean full and strong!
So well and bravely has he done the work be found to do,
To justice, freedom, duty, God, and man forever true.

—WHITTIER.

JOHN QUINCY ADAMS AND THE RIGHT OF PETITION

The lot of ex-Presidents of the United States, as a rule, has been a life of extreme retirement, but to this rule there is one marked exception. When John Quincy Adams left the White House in March, 1829, it must have seemed as if public life could hold nothing more for him.

He had had everything apparently that an American statesman could hope for. He had been Minister to Holland and Prussia, to Russia and England.

He had been a Senator of the United States, Secretary of State for eight years, and finally President. Yet, notwithstanding all this, the greatest part of his career, and his noblest service to his country, were still before him when he gave up the Presidency.

In the following year (1830) he was told that he might be elected to the House of Representatives, and the gentleman who made the proposition ventured to say that he thought an ex-President, by taking such a position, "instead of degrading the individual would elevate the representative character." Mr. Adams replied that he had "in that respect no scruples whatever. No person can be degraded by serving the people as Representative in Congress, nor, in my opinion, would an ex-President of the United States be degraded by serving as a selectman of his town if elected thereto by the people." A few weeks later he was chosen to the House, and the district continued to send him every two years from that time until his death. He did much excellent work in the House, and was conspicuous in more than one memorable scene; but here it is possible to touch on only a single point, where he came forward as the champion of a great principle, and fought a battle for the right which will always be remembered among the great deeds of American public men.

Soon after Mr. Adams took his seat in Congress, the movement for the abolition of slavery was begun by a few obscure agitators. It did not at first attract much attention, but as it went on it gradually exasperated the overbearing temper of the Southern slaveholders. One fruit of this agitation was the appearance of petitions for the abolition of slavery in the House of Representatives. A few were presented by Mr. Adams without attracting much notice; but as the petitions multiplied, the Southern representatives became aroused. They assailed Mr. Adams for presenting them, and finally passed what was known as the gag rule, which prevented the reception of these petitions by the House. Against this rule Mr. Adams protested, in the midst of the loud shouts of the Southerners, as a violation of his constitutional rights. But the tyranny of slavery at that time was so complete that the rule was adopted and enforced, and the slave-holders, undertook in this way to suppress free speech in the House, just as they also undertook to prevent the transmission through the mails of any writings adverse to slavery. With the wisdom of a statesman and a man of affairs, Mr. Adams addressed himself to the one practical point of the contest. He did not enter upon a discussion of slavery or of its abolition, but turned his whole force toward the vindication of the right of petition. On every petition day he would offer, in constantly increasing numbers, petitions which came to him from all parts of the country for the abolition of slavery, in this way driving the Southern representatives almost to madness, despite their rule which prevented the reception of such documents when offered. Their hatred of Mr. Adams is something difficult to conceive, and they were burning to break him down, and, if possible, drive him from the House. On February 6, 1837, after presenting the usual petitions, Mr. Adams offered one upon which he said he should like the judgment of the Speaker as to its propriety, inasmuch as it was a petition from slaves. In a moment the House was in a tumult, and loud cries of "Expel him!" "Expel him!" rose in all directions. One resolution after another was offered looking toward his expulsion or censure, and it was not until February 9, three days later, that he was able to take the floor in his own defense. His speech was a masterpiece of argument, invective, and sarcasm. He showed, among other things, that he had not offered the petition, but had only asked the opinion of the Speaker upon it, and that the petition itself prayed that slavery should not be abolished. When he closed his speech, which was quite as savage as any made against him, and infinitely abler, no one desired to reply, and the idea of censuring him was dropped.

The greatest struggle, however, came five years later, when, on January 21, 1842, Mr. Adams presented the petition of certain citizens of Haverhill, Massachusetts, praying for the dissolution of the Union on account of slavery. His enemies felt that now, at last, he had delivered himself into their hands. Again arose the cry for his expulsion, and again vituperation was poured out upon him, and resolutions to expel him freely introduced. When he got the floor to speak in his own defense, he faced an excited House, almost unanimously hostile to him, and possessing, as he well knew, both the will and the power to drive him from its walls. But there was no wavering in Mr. Adams. "If they say they will try me," he said, "they must try me. If they say they will punish me, they must punish me. But if they say that in peace and mercy they will spare me expulsion, I disdain and cast away their mercy, and I ask if they will come to such a trial and expel me. I defy them. I have constituents to go to, and they will have something to say if this House expels me, nor will it be long before the gentlemen will see me here again." The fight went on for nearly a fortnight, and on February 7 the whole subject was finally laid on the table. The sturdy, dogged fighter, single-handed and alone, had beaten all the forces of the South and of slavery. No more memorable fight has ever been made by one man in a parliamentary body, and after this decisive struggle the tide began to turn. Every year Mr. Adams renewed his motion to strike out the gag rule, and forced it to a vote. Gradually the majority against it dwindled, until at last, on December 3, 1844, his motion prevailed. Freedom of speech had been vindicated in the American House of Representatives, the right of petition had been won, and the first great blow against the slave power had been struck.

Four years later Mr. Adams fell, stricken with paralysis, at his place in the House, and a few hours afterward, with the words, "This is the last of earth; I am content," upon his lips, he sank into unconsciousness and died. It was a fit end to a great public career. His fight for the right of petition is one to be studied and remembered, and Mr. Adams made it practically alone. The slaveholders of the South and the representatives of the North were alike against him. Against him, too, as his biographer, Mr. Morse, says, was the class in Boston to which he naturally belonged by birth and education. He had to encounter the bitter resistance in his own set of the "conscienceless respectability of wealth," but the great body of the New England people were with him, as were the voters of his own district. He was an old man, with the physical infirmities of age. His eyes were weak and streaming; his hands were trembling; his voice cracked in moments of excitement; yet in that age of oratory, in the days of Webster and Clay, he was known as the "old man eloquent." It was what he said, more than the way he said it, which told. His vigorous mind never worked more surely and clearly than when he stood alone in the midst of an angry House, the target of their hatred and abuse. His arguments were strong, and his large knowledge and wide experience supplied him with every weapon for defense and attack. Beneath the lash of his invective and his sarcasm the hottest of the slaveholders cowered away. He set his back against a great principle. He never retreated an inch, he never yielded, he never conciliated, he was always an assailant, and no man and no body of men had the power to turn him. He had his dark hours, he felt bitterly the isolation of his position, but he never swerved. He had good right to set down in his diary, when the gag rule was repealed, "Blessed, forever blessed, be the name of God."

FRANCIS PARKMAN
(1822–1893)

He told the red man's story; far and wide
    He searched the unwritten annals of his race;
He sat a listener at the Sachem's side,
    He tracked the hunter through his wild-wood chase.

High o'er his head the soaring eagle screamed;
    The wolf's long howl rang nightly; through the vale
Tramped the lone bear; the panther's eyeballs gleamed;
    The bison's gallop thundered on the gale.

Soon o'er the horizon rose the cloud of strife,
    Two proud, strong nations battling for the prize:
Which swarming host should mould a nation's life;
    Which royal banner flout the western skies.

Long raged the conflict; on the crimson sod
    Native and alien joined their hosts in vain;
The lilies withered where the lion trod,
    Till Peace lay panting on the ravaged plain.

A nobler task was theirs who strove to win
    The blood-stained heathen to the Christian fold;
To free from Satan's clutch the slaves of sin;
    These labors, too, with loving grace he told.

Halting with feeble step, or bending o'er
    The sweet-breathed roses which he loved so well,
While through long years his burdening cross he bore,
    From those firm lips no coward accents fell.

A brave bright memory! His the stainless shield
    No shame defaces and no envy mars!
When our far future's record is unsealed,
    His name will shine among its morning stars.

                                —Holmes.

FRANCIS PARKMAN (1822–1893)

The stories in this volume deal, for the most part, with single actions, generally with deeds of war and feats of arms. In this one I desire to give if possible the impression, for it can be no more than an impression, of a life which in its conflicts and its victories manifested throughout heroic qualities. Such qualities can be shown in many ways, and the field of battle is only one of the fields of human endeavor where heroism can be displayed.

Francis Parkman was born in Boston on September 16, 1822. He came of a well-known family, and was of a good Puritan stock. He was rather a delicate boy, with an extremely active mind and of a highly sensitive, nervous organization. Into everything that attracted him he threw himself with feverish energy. His first passion, when he was only about twelve years old, was for chemistry, and his eager boyish experiments in this direction were undoubtedly injurious to his health. The interest in chemistry was succeeded by a passion for the woods and the wilderness, and out of this came the longing to write the history of the men of the wilderness, and of the great struggle between France and England for the control of the North American continent. All through his college career this desire was with him, and while in secret he was reading widely to prepare himself for his task, he also spent a great deal of time in the forests and on the mountains. To quote his own words, he was "fond of hardships, and he was vain of enduring them, cherishing a sovereign scorn for every physical weakness or defect; but deceived, moreover, by the rapid development of frame and sinew, which flattered him into the belief that discipline sufficiently unsparing would harden him into an athlete, he slighted the precautions of a more reasonable woodcraft, tired old foresters with long marches, stopped neither for heat nor for rain, and slept on the earth without blankets." The result was that his intense energy carried him beyond his strength, and while his muscles strengthened and hardened, his sensitive nervous organization began to give way. It was not merely because he led an active outdoor life. He himself protests against any such conclusion, and says that "if any pale student glued to his desk here seek an apology for a way of life whose natural fruit is that pallid and emasculate scholarship, of which New England has had too many examples, it will be far better that this sketch had not been written. For the student there is, in its season, no better place than the saddle, and no better companion than the rifle or the oar."

The evil that was done was due to Parkman's highly irritable organism, which spurred him to excess in everything he undertook. The first special sign of the mischief he was doing to himself and his health appeared in a weakness of sight. It was essential to his plan of historical work to study not only books and records but Indian life from the inside. Therefore, having graduated from college and the law-school, he felt that the time had come for this investigation, which would enable him to gather material for his history and at the same time to rest his eyes. He went to the Rocky Mountains, and after great hardships, living in the saddle, as he said, with weakness and pain, he joined a band of Ogallalla Indians. With them he remained despite his physical suffering, and from them he learned, as he could not have learned in any other way, what Indian life really was.

The immediate result of the journey was his first book, instinct with the freshness and wildness of the mountains and the prairies, and called by him "The Oregon Trail." Unfortunately, the book was not the only outcome. The illness incurred during his journey from fatigue and exposure was followed by other disorders. The light of the sun became insupportable, and his nervous system was entirely deranged. His sight was now so impaired that he was almost blind, and could neither read nor write. It was a terrible prospect for a brilliant and ambitious man, but Parkman faced it unflinchingly. He devised a frame by which he could write with closed eyes, and books and manuscripts were read to him. In this way he began the history of "The Conspiracy of Pontiac," and for the first half-year the rate of composition covered about six lines a day. His courage was rewarded by an improvement in his health, and a little more quiet in nerves and brain. In two and a half years he managed to complete the book. He then entered upon his great subject of "France in the New World." The material was mostly in manuscript, and had to be examined, gathered, and selected in Europe and in Canada.

He could not read, he could write only a very little and that with difficulty, and yet he pressed on. He slowly collected his material and digested and arranged it, using the eyes of others to do that which he could not do himself, and always on the verge of a complete breakdown of mind and body. In 1851 he had an effusion of water on the left knee, which stopped his outdoor exercise, on which he had always largely depended. All the irritability of the system then centered in the head, resulting in intense pain and in a restless and devouring activity of thought. He himself says: "The whirl, the confusion, and strange, undefined tortures attending this condition are only to be conceived by one who has felt them." The resources of surgery and medicine were exhausted in vain. The trouble in the head and eyes constantly recurred.

In 1858 there came a period when for four years he was incapable of the slightest mental application, and the attacks varied in duration from four hours to as many months. When the pressure was lightened a little he went back to his work. When work was impossible, he turned to horticulture, grew roses, and wrote a book about the cultivation of those flowers which is a standard authority.

As he grew older the attacks moderated, although they

never departed. Sleeplessness pursued him always, the slightest excitement would deprive him of the power of exertion, his sight was always sensitive, and at times he was bordering on blindness. In this hard-pressed way he fought the battle of life. He says himself that his books took four times as long to prepare and write as if he had been strong and able to use his faculties. That this should have been the case is little wonder, for those books came into being with failing sight and shattered nerves, with sleeplessness and pain, and the menace of insanity ever hanging over the brave man who, nevertheless, carried them through to an end.

Yet the result of those fifty years, even in amount, is a noble one, and would have been great achievement for a man who had never known a sick day. In quality, and subject, and method of narration, they leave little to be desired. There, in Parkman's volumes, is told vividly, strongly, and truthfully, the history of the great struggle between France and England for the mastery of the North American continent, one of the most important events of modern times. This is not the place to give any critical estimate of Mr. Parkman's work. It is enough to say that it stands in the front rank. It is a great contribution to history, and a still greater gift to the literature of this country. All Americans certainly should read the volumes in which Parkman has told that wonderful story of hardship and adventure, of fighting and of statesmanship, which gave this great continent to the English race and the English speech. But better than the literature or the history is the heroic spirit of the man, which triumphed over pain and all other physical obstacles, and brought a work of such value to his country and his time into existence. There is a great lesson as well as a lofty example in such a career, and in the service which such a man rendered by his life and work to literature and to his country. On the tomb of the conqueror of Quebec it is written: "Here lies Wolfe victorious."

The same epitaph might with entire justice be carved above the grave of Wolfe's historian.

"REMEMBER
THE ALAMO"

The muffled drum's sad roll has beat
    The soldier's last tattoo;
No more on life's parade shall meet
    That brave and fallen few.
On fame's eternal camping-ground
    Their silent tents are spread,
And glory guards with solemn round
    The bivouac of the dead.

* * *

The neighing troop, the flashing blade,
    The bugle's stirring blast,
The charge, the dreadful cannonade,
    The din and shout are past;
Nor war's wild note, nor glory's peal
    Shall thrill with fierce delight
Those breasts that never more may feel
    The rapture of the fight.

—THEODORE O'HARA.

"REMEMBER THE ALAMO"

"Thermopylae had its messengers of death, but the Alamo had none." These were the words with which a United States senator referred to one of the most resolute and effective fights ever waged by brave men against overwhelming odds in the face of certain death.

Soon after the close of the second war with Great Britain, parties of American settlers began to press forward into the rich, sparsely settled territory of Texas, then a portion of Mexico. At first these immigrants were well received, but the Mexicans speedily grew jealous of them, and oppressed them in various ways. In consequence, when the settlers felt themselves strong enough, they revolted against Mexican rule, and declared Texas to be an independent republic. Immediately Santa Anna, the Dictator of Mexico, gathered a large army, and invaded Texas. The slender forces of the settlers were unable to meet his hosts. They were pressed back by the Mexicans, and dreadful atrocities were committed by Santa Anna and his lieutenants. In the United States there was great enthusiasm for the struggling Texans, and many bold backwoodsmen and Indian-fighters swarmed to their help. Among them the two most famous were Sam Houston and David Crockett. Houston was the younger man, and had already led an extraordinary and varied career. When a mere lad he had run away from home and joined the Cherokees, living among them for some years; then he returned home. He had fought under Andrew Jackson in his campaigns against the Creeks, and had been severely wounded at the battle of the Horse-shoe Bend. He had risen to the highest political honors in his State, becoming governor of Tennessee; and then suddenly, in a fit of moody longing for the life of the wilderness, he gave up his governorship, left the State, and crossed the Mississippi, going to join his old comrades, the Cherokees, in their new home along the waters of the Arkansas. Here he dressed, lived, fought, hunted, and drank precisely like any Indian, becoming one of the chiefs.

David Crockett was born soon after the Revolutionary War. He, too, had taken part under Jackson in the campaigns against the Creeks, and had afterward become a man of mark in Tennessee, and gone to Congress as a Whig; but he had quarreled with Jackson, and been beaten for Congress, and in his disgust he left the State and decided to join the Texans. He was the most famous rifle-shot in all the United States, and the most successful hunter, so that his skill was a proverb all along the border.

David Crockett journeyed south, by boat and horse, making his way steadily toward the distant plains where the Texans were waging their life-and-death fight. Texas was a wild place in those days, and the old hunter had more than one hairbreadth escape from Indians, desperadoes, and savage beasts, ere he got to the neighborhood of San Antonio, and joined another adventurer, a bee-hunter, bent on the same errand as himself. The two had been in ignorance of exactly what the situation in Texas was; but they soon found that the Mexican army was marching toward San Antonio, whither they were going. Near the town was an old Spanish fort, the Alamo, in which the hundred and fifty American defenders of the place had gathered. Santa Anna had four thousand troops with him. The Alamo was a mere shell, utterly unable to withstand either a bombardment or a regular assault. It was evident, therefore, that those within it would be in the utmost jeopardy if the place were seriously assaulted, but old Crockett and his companion never wavered. They were fearless and resolute, and masters of woodcraft, and they managed to slip through the Mexican lines and join the defenders within the walls.

The bravest, the hardiest, the most reckless men of the border were there; among them were Colonel Travis, the commander of the fort, and Bowie, the inventor of the famous bowie-knife. They were a wild and ill-disciplined band, little used to restraint or control, but they were men of iron courage and great bodily powers, skilled in the use of their weapons, and ready to meet with stern and uncomplaining indifference whatever doom fate might have in store for them.

Soon Santa Anna approached with his army, took possession of the town, and besieged the fort. The defenders knew there was scarcely a chance of rescue, and that it was hopeless to expect that one hundred and fifty men, behind defenses so weak, could beat off four thousand trained soldiers, well armed and provided with heavy artillery; but they had no idea of flinching, and made a desperate defense. The days went by, and no help came, while Santa Anna got ready his lines, and began a furious cannonade. His gunners were unskilled, however, and he had to serve the guns from a distance; for when they were pushed nearer, the American riflemen crept forward under cover, and picked off the artillerymen.

Old Crockett thus killed five men at one gun. But, by degrees, the bombardment told. The walls of the Alamo were battered and riddled; and when they had been breached so as to afford no obstacle to the rush of his soldiers, Santa Anna commanded that they be stormed.

The storm took place on March 6, 1836. The Mexican troops came on well and steadily, breaking through the outer defenses at every point, for the lines were too long to be manned by the few Americans. The frontiersmen then retreated to the inner building, and a desperate hand-to-hand conflict followed, the Mexicans thronging in, shooting the Americans with their muskets, and thrusting at them with lance and bayonet, while the Americans, after firing their long rifles, clubbed them, and fought desperately, one against many; and they also used their bowie-knives and revolvers with deadly effect. The fight reeled to and fro between the shattered walls, each American the center of a group of foes; but, for all their strength and their wild fighting courage, the defenders were too few, and the struggle could have but one end. One by one the tall riflemen succumbed, after repeated thrusts with bayonet and lance, until but three or four were left. Colonel Travis, the commander, was among them; and so was Bowie, who was sick and weak from a wasting disease, but who rallied all his strength to die fighting, and who, in the final struggle, slew several Mexicans with his revolver, and with his big knife of the kind to which he had given his name. Then these fell too, and the last man stood at bay. It was old Davy Crockett.

Wounded in a dozen places, he faced his foes with his back to the wall, ringed around by the bodies of the men he had slain. So desperate was the fight he waged, that the Mexicans who thronged round about him were beaten back for the moment, and no one dared to run in upon him.

Accordingly, while the lancers held him where he was, for, weakened by wounds and loss of blood, he could not break through them, the musketeers loaded their carbines and shot him down. Santa Anna declined to give him mercy. Some say that when Crockett fell from his wounds, he was taken alive, and was then shot by Santa Anna's order; but his fate cannot be told with certainty, for not a single American was left alive.

At any rate, after Crockett fell the fight was over. Every one of the hardy men who had held the Alamo lay still in death. Yet they died well avenged, for four times their number fell at their hands in the battle.

Santa Anna had but a short while in which to exult over his bloody and hard-won victory. Already a rider from the rolling Texas plains, going north through the Indian Territory, had told Houston that the Texans were up and were striving for their liberty. At once in Houston's mind there kindled a longing to return to the men of his race at the time of their need. Mounting his horse, he rode south by night and day, and was hailed by the Texans as a heaven-sent leader. He took command of their forces, eleven hundred stark riflemen, and at the battle of San Jacinto, he and his men charged the Mexican hosts with the cry of "Remember the Alamo." Almost immediately, the Mexicans were overthrown with terrible slaughter; Santa Anna himself was captured, and the freedom of Texas was won at a blow.

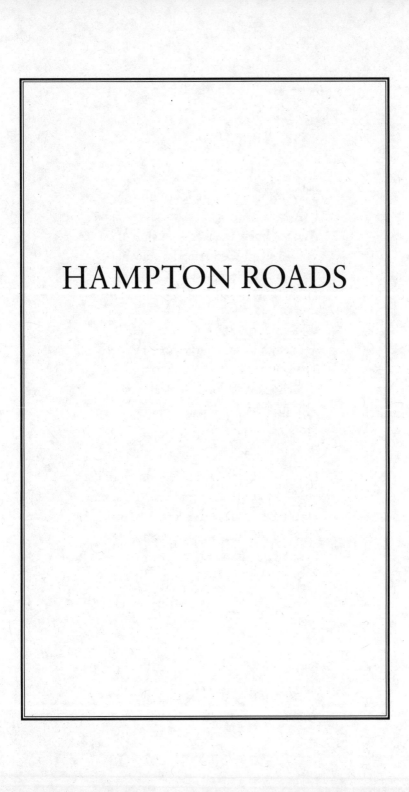

HAMPTON ROADS

Then far away to the south uprose
   A little feather of snow-white smoke,
And we knew that the iron ship of our foes
   Was steadily steering its course
   To try the force
Of our ribs of oak.

Down upon us heavily runs,
   Silent and sullen, the floating fort;
Then comes a puff of smoke from her guns,
   And leaps the terrible death,
   With fiery breath,
From her open port.

* * *

Ho! brave hearts, that went down in the seas!
   Ye are at peace in the troubled stream;
Ho! brave land! with hearts like these,
   Thy flag, that is rent in twain,
   Shall be one again,
And without a seam!

—LONGFELLOW.

HAMPTON ROADS

The naval battles of the Civil War possess an immense importance, because they mark the line of cleavage between naval warfare under the old, and naval warfare under the new, conditions. The ships with which Hull and Decatur and McDonough won glory in the war of 1812 were essentially like those with which Drake and Hawkins and Frobisher had harried the Spanish armadas two centuries and a half earlier. They were wooden sailing-vessels, carrying many guns mounted in broadside, like those of De Ruyter and Tromp, of Blake and Nelson. Throughout this period all the great admirals, all the famous single-ship fighters,—whose skill reached its highest expression in our own navy during the war of 1812,—commanded craft built and armed in a substantially similar manner, and fought with the same weapons and under much the same conditions. But in the Civil War weapons and methods were introduced which caused a revolution greater even than that which divided the sailing-ship from the galley. The use of steam, the casing of ships in iron armor, and the employment of the torpedo, the ram, and the gun of high power, produced such radically new types that the old ships of the line became at one stroke as antiquated as the galleys of Hamilcar or Alcibiades. Some of these new engines of destruction were invented, and all were for the first time tried in actual combat, during our own Civil War. The first occasion on which any of the new methods were thoroughly tested was attended by incidents which made it one of the most striking of naval battles.

In Chesapeake Bay, near Hampton Roads, the United States had collected a fleet of wooden ships; some of them old-style sailing-vessels, others steamers. The Confederates were known to be building a great iron-clad ram, and the wooden vessels were eagerly watching for her appearance when she should come out of Gosport Harbor. Her powers and capacity were utterly unknown. She was made out of the former United States steam-frigate Merrimac, cut down so as to make her fore and aft decks nearly flat, and not much above the water, while the guns were mounted in a covered central battery, with sloping flanks. Her sides, deck, and battery were coated with iron, and she was armed with formidable rifle-guns, and, most important of all, with a steel ram thrust out under water forward from her bow. She was commanded by a gallant and efficient officer, Captain Buchanan.

It was March 8, 1862, when the ram at last made her appearance within sight of the Union fleet. The day was calm and very clear, so that the throngs of spectators on shore could see every feature of the battle.

With the great ram came three light gunboats, all of which took part in the action, harassing the vessels which she assailed; but they were not factors of importance in the fight. On the Union side the vessels nearest were the sailing-ships Cumberland and Congress, and the steam-frigate Minnesota. The Congress and Cumberland were anchored not far from each other; the Minnesota got aground, and was some distance off. Owing to the currents and shoals and the lack of wind, no other vessel was able to get up in time to take a part in the fight.

As soon as the ram appeared out of the harbor, she turned and steamed toward the Congress and the Cumberland, the black smoke rising from her funnels, and the great ripples running from each side of her iron prow as she drove steadily through the still waters. On board of the Congress and Cumberland there was eager anticipation, but not a particle of fear.

The officers in command, Captain Smith and Lieutenant Morris, were two of the most gallant men in a service where gallantry has always been too common to need special comment. The crews were composed of veterans, well trained, self-confident, and proud beyond measure of the flag whose honor they upheld. The guns were run out, and the men stood at quarters, while the officers eagerly conned the approaching ironclad. The Congress was the first to open fire; and, as her volleys flew, the men on the Cumberland were astounded to see the cannon-shot bound off the sloping sides of the ram as hailstones bound from a windowpane. The ram answered, and her rifle-shells tore the sides of the Congress; but for her first victim she aimed at the Cumberland, and, firing her bow guns, came straight as an arrow at the little sloop-of-war, which lay broadside to her.

It was an absolutely hopeless struggle. The Cumberland was a sailing-ship, at anchor, with wooden sides, and a battery of light guns. Against the formidable steam ironclad, with her heavy rifles and steel ram, she was as powerless as if she had been a rowboat; and from the moment the men saw the cannon-shot bound from the ram's sides they knew they were doomed. But none of them flinched. Once and again they fired their guns full against the approaching ram, and in response received a few shells from the great bow-rifles of the latter. Then, forging ahead, the Merrimac struck her antagonist with her steel prow, and the sloop-of-war reeled and shuddered, and through the great rent in her side the black water rushed. She foundered in a few minutes; but her crew fought her to the last, cheering as they ran out the guns, and sending shot after shot against the ram as the latter backed off after delivering her blow. The rush of the water soon swamped the lower decks, but the men above continued to serve their guns until the upper deck also was awash, and the vessel had not ten seconds of life left. Then, with her flags flying, her men cheering, and her guns firing, the Cumberland sank. It was shallow where she settled down, so that her masts remained above the water. The glorious flag for which the brave men aboard her had died flew proudly in the wind all that day, while the fight went on, and throughout the night; and next morning it was still streaming over the beautiful bay, to mark the resting-place of as gallant a vessel as ever sailed or fought on the high seas.

After the Cumberland sank, the ram turned her attention to the Congress. Finding it difficult to get to her in the shoal water, she began to knock her to pieces with her great rifle-guns. The unequal fight between the ironclad and the wooden ship lasted for perhaps half an hour. By that time the commander of the Congress had been killed, and her decks looked like a slaughter-house. She was utterly unable to make any impression on her foe, and finally she took fire and blew up. The Minnesota was the third victim marked for destruction, and the Merrimac began the attack upon her at once; but it was getting very late, and as the water was shoal and she could not get close, the rain finally drew back to her anchorage, to wait until next day before renewing and completing her work of destruction.

All that night there was the wildest exultation among the Confederates, while the gloom and panic of the Union men cannot be described. It was evident that the United States ships-of-war were as helpless as cockle-shells against their iron-clad foe, and there was no question but that she could destroy the whole fleet with ease and with absolute impunity. This meant not only the breaking of the blockade; but the sweeping away at one blow of the North's naval supremacy, which was indispensable to the success of the war for the Union. It is small wonder that during that night the wisest and bravest should have almost despaired.

But in the hour of the nation's greatest need a champion suddenly appeared, in time to play the last scene in this great drama of sea warfare. The North, too, had been trying its hand at building ironclads.

The most successful of them was the little Monitor, a flat-decked, low, turreted, ironclad, armed with a couple of heavy guns. She was the first experiment of her kind, and her absolutely flat surface, nearly level with the water, her revolving turret, and her utter unlikeness to any pre-existing naval type, had made her an object of mirth among most practical seamen; but her inventor, Ericsson, was not disheartened in the least by the jeers. Under the command of a gallant naval officer, Captain Worden, she was sent South from New York, and though she almost foundered in a gale she managed to weather it, and reached the scene of the battle at Hampton Roads at the moment when her presence was all-important.

Early the following morning the Merrimac, now under Captain Jones (for Buchanan had been wounded), again steamed forth to take up the work she had so well begun and to destroy the Union fleet. She steered straight for the Minnesota; but when she was almost there, to her astonishment a strange-looking little craft advanced from the side of the big wooden frigate and boldly barred the Merrimac's path. For a moment the Confederates could hardly believe their eyes. The Monitor was tiny, compared to their ship, for she was not one fifth the size, and her queer appearance made them look at their new foe with contempt; but the first shock of battle did away with this feeling. The Merrimac turned on her foe her rifleguns, intending to blow her out of the water, but the shot glanced from the thick iron turret of the Monitor. Then the Monitors guns opened fire, and as the great balls struck the sides of the ram her plates started and her timbers gave. Had the Monitor been such a vessel as those of her type produced later in the war, the ram would have been sunk then and there; but as it was her shot were not quite heavy enough to pierce the iron walls. Around and around the two strange combatants hovered, their guns bellowing without cessation, while the men on the frigates and on shore watched the result with breathless interest. Neither the Merrimac nor the Monitor could dispose of its antagonist. The ram's guns could not damage the turret, and the Monitor was able dexterously to avoid the stroke of the formidable prow. On the other hand, the shot of the Monitor could not penetrate the Merrimac's tough sides. Accordingly, fierce though the struggle was, and much though there was that hinged on it, it was not bloody in character.

The Merrimac could neither destroy nor evade the Monitor. She could not sink her when she tried to, and when she abandoned her and turned to attack one of the other wooden vessels, the little turreted ship was thrown across her path, so that the fight had to be renewed. Both sides grew thoroughly exhausted, and finally the battle ceased by mutual consent.

Nothing more could be done. The ram was badly damaged, and there was no help for her save to put back to the port whence she had come. Twice afterward she came out, but neither time did she come near enough to the Monitor to attack her, and the latter could not move off where she would cease to protect the wooden vessels. The ram was ultimately blown up by the Confederates on the advance of the Union army.

Tactically, the fight was a drawn battle—neither ship being able to damage the other, and both ships, being fought to a standstill; but the moral and material effects were wholly in favor of the Monitor. Her victory was hailed with exultant joy throughout the whole Union, and exercised a correspondingly depressing effect in the Confederacy; while every naval man throughout the world, who possessed eyes to see, saw that the fight in Hampton Roads had inaugurated a new era in ocean warfare, and that the Monitor and Merrimac, which had waged so gallant and so terrible a battle, were the first ships of the new era, and that as such their names would be forever famous.

THE
FLAG-BEARER

Mine eyes have seen the glory of the coming of the Lord;
He is trampling out the vintage where the grapes of wrath are
   stored;
He hath loosed the fateful lightning of His terrible swift sword;
   His truth is marching on.

I have seen Him in the watch-fires of a hundred circling camps;
They have builded Him an altar in the evening dews and damps;
I can read his righteous sentence by the dim and flaring lamps;
   His day is marching on.
He has sounded forth the trumpet that shall never beat retreat;
He is sifting out the hearts of men before his judgment seat;
Oh! be swift, my soul, to answer him! be jubilant, my feet!
   Our God is marching on.

—Julia Ward Howe.

THE FLAG-BEARER

In no war since the close of the great Napoleonic struggles has the fighting been so obstinate and bloody as in the Civil War. Much has been said in song and story of the resolute courage of the Guards at Inkerman, of the charge of the Light Brigade, and of the terrible fighting and loss of the German armies at Mars La Tour and Gravelotte.

The praise bestowed, upon the British and Germans for their valor, and for the loss that proved their valor, was well deserved; but there were over one hundred and twenty regiments, Union and Confederate, each of which, in some one battle of the Civil War, suffered a greater loss than any English regiment at Inkerman or at any other battle in the Crimea, a greater loss than was suffered by any German regiment at Gravelotte or at any other battle of the Franco-Prussian war. No European regiment in any recent struggle has suffered such losses as at Gettysburg befell the 1st Minnesota, when 82 percent of the officers and men were killed and wounded; or the 141st Pennsylvania, which lost 76 percent; or the 26th North Carolina, which lost 72 percent; such as at the second battle of Manassas befell the 101st New York, which lost 74 percent, and the 21st Georgia, which lost

76 percent. At Cold Harbor the 25th Massachusetts lost 70 percent, and the 10th Tennessee at Chickamauga 68 percent; while at Shiloh the 9th Illinois lost 63 percent, and the 6th Mississippi 70 percent; and at Antietam the 1st Texas lost 82 percent. The loss of the Light Brigade in killed and wounded in its famous charge at Balaklava was but 37 percent.

These figures show the terrible punishment endured by these regiments, chosen at random from the head of the list which shows the slaughter-roll of the Civil War. Yet the shattered remnants of each regiment preserved their organization, and many of the severest losses were incurred in the hour of triumph, and not of disaster. Thus, the 1st Minnesota, at Gettysburg, suffered its appalling loss while charging a greatly superior force, which it drove before it; and the little huddle of wounded and unwounded men who survived their victorious charge actually kept both the flag they had captured and the ground from which they had driven their foes.

A number of the Continental regiments under Washington, Greene, and Wayne did valiant fighting and endured heavy punishment. Several of the regiments raised on the northern frontier in 1814 showed, under Brown and Scott, that they were able to meet the best troops of Britain on equal terms in the open, and even to overmatch them in fair fight with the bayonet. The regiments which, in the Mexican war, under the lead of Taylor, captured Monterey, and beat back Santa Anna at Buena Vista, or which, with Scott as commander, stormed Molino Del

Rey and Chapultepec, proved their ability to bear terrible loss, to wrest victory from overwhelming numbers, and to carry by open assault positions of formidable strength held by a veteran army. But in none of these three wars was the fighting so resolute and bloody as in the Civil War.

Countless deeds of heroism were performed by Northerner and by Southerner, by officer and by private, in every year of the great struggle. The immense majority of these deeds went unrecorded, and were known to few beyond the immediate participants. Of those that were noticed it would be impossible even to make a dry catalogue in ten such volumes as this. All that can be done is to choose out two or three acts of heroism, not as exceptions, but as examples of hundreds of others.

The times of war are iron times, and bring out all that is best as well as all that is basest in the human heart. In a full recital of the civil war, as of every other great conflict, there would stand out in naked relief feats of wonderful daring and self-devotion, and, mixed among them, deeds of cowardice, of treachery, of barbarous brutality. Sadder still, such a recital would show strange contrasts in the careers of individual men, men who at one time acted well and nobly, and at another time ill and basely. The ugly truths must not be blinked, and the lessons they teach should be set forth by every historian, and learned by every statesman and soldier; but, for our good fortune, the lessons best worth learning in the nation's past are lessons of heroism.

From immemorial time the armies of every warlike people have set the highest value upon the standards they bore to battle. To guard one's own flag against capture is the pride, to capture the flag of one's enemy the ambition, of every valiant soldier. In consequence, in every war between peoples of good military record, feats of daring performed by color-bearers are honorably common. The Civil War was full of such incidents. Out of very many two or three may be mentioned as noteworthy.

One occurred at Fredericksburg on the day when half the brigades of Meagher and Caldwell lay on the bloody slope leading up to the Confederate entrenchments. Among the assaulting regiments was the 5th New Hampshire, and it lost one hundred and eighty-six out of three hundred men who made the charge. The survivors fell sullenly back behind a fence, within easy range of the Confederate rifle-pits. Just before reaching it the last of the color guard was shot, and the flag fell in the open. A Captain Perry instantly ran out to rescue it, and as he reached it was shot through the heart; another, Captain Murray, made the same attempt and was also killed; and so was a third, Moore. Several private soldiers met a like fate. They were all killed close to the flag, and their dead bodies fell across one another. Taking advantage of this breastwork, Lieutenant Nettleton crawled from behind the fence to the colors, seized them, and bore back the blood-won trophy.

Another took place at Gaines' Mill, where Gregg's 1st South Carolina formed part of the attacking force.

The resistance was desperate, and the fury of the assault unsurpassed. At one point it fell to the lot of this regiment to bear the brunt of carrying a certain strong position.

Moving forward at a run, the South Carolinians were swept by a fierce and searching fire. Young James Taylor, a lad of sixteen, was carrying the flag, and was killed after being shot down three times, twice rising and struggling onward with the colors. The third time he fell the flag was seized by George Cotchet, and when he, in turn, fell, by Shubrick Hayne. Hayne was also struck down almost immediately, and the fourth lad, for none of them were over twenty years old, grasped the colors, and fell mortally wounded across the body of his friend. The fifth, Gadsden Holmes, was pierced with no less than seven balls. The sixth man, Dominick Spellman, more fortunate, but not less brave, bore the flag throughout the rest of the battle.

Yet another occurred at Antietam. The 7th Maine, then under the command of Major T. W. Hyde, was one of the hundreds of regiments that on many hard-fought fields established a reputation for dash and unyielding endurance. Toward the early part of the day at Antietam it merely took its share in the charging and long-range firing, together with the New York and Vermont regiments which were its immediate neighbors in the line. The fighting was very heavy. In one of the charges, the Maine men passed over what had been a Confederate regiment. The gray-clad soldiers were lying, both ranks, privates and officers, as they fell, for so many had been killed or disabled that it seemed as if the whole regiment was prone in death.

Much of the time the Maine men lay on the battle-field, hugging the ground, under a heavy artillery fire, but beyond the reach of ordinary musketry. One of the privates, named Knox, was a wonderful shot, and had received permission to use his own special rifle, a weapon accurately sighted for very long range. While the regiment thus lay under the storm of shot and shell, he asked leave to go to the front; and for an hour afterward his companions heard his rifle crack every few minutes. Major Hyde finally, from curiosity, crept forward to see what he was doing, and found that he had driven every man away from one section of a Confederate battery, tumbling over gunner after gunner as they came forward to fire. One of his victims was a general officer, whose horse he killed. At the end of an hour or so, a piece of shell took off the breech of his pet rifle, and he returned disconsolate; but after a few minutes he gathered three rifles that were left by wounded men, and went back again to his work.

At five o'clock in the afternoon the regiment was suddenly called upon to undertake a hopeless charge, owing to the blunder of the brigade commander, who was a gallant veteran of the Mexican war, but who was also given to drink. Opposite the Union lines at this point were some haystacks, near a group of farm buildings. They were right in the center of the Confederate position, and sharpshooters stationed among them were picking off the Union gunners. The brigadier, thinking that they were held by but a few skirmishers, rode to where the 7th Maine was lying on the ground, and said: "Major Hyde, take your regiment and drive the enemy from those trees and buildings." Hyde saluted, and said that he had seen a large force of rebels go in among the buildings, probably two brigades in all. The brigadier answered, "Are you afraid to go, sir?" and repeated the order emphatically. "Give the order, so the regiment can hear it, and we are ready, sir," said Hyde. This was done, and "Attention" brought every man to his feet. With the regiment were two young boys who carried the marking guidons, and Hyde ordered these to the rear. They pretended to go, but as soon as the regiment charged came along with it. One of them lost his arm, and the other was killed on the field. The colors were carried by the color corporal, Harry Campbell.

Hyde gave the orders to left face and forward and the Maine men marched out in front of a Vermont regiment which lay beside them; then, facing to the front, they crossed a sunken road, which was so filled with dead and wounded Confederates that Hyde's horse had to step on them to get over.

Once across, they stopped for a moment in the trampled corn to straighten the line, and then charged toward the right of the barns.

On they went at the double-quick, fifteen skirmishers ahead under Lieutenant Butler, Major Hyde on the right on his Virginia thoroughbred, and Adjutant Haskell to the left on a big white horse. The latter was shot down at once, as was his horse, and Hyde rode round in front of the regiment just in time to see a long line of men in gray rise from behind the stone wall of the Hagerstown pike, which was to their right, and pour in a volley; but it mostly went too high. He then ordered his men to left oblique.

Just as they were abreast a hill to the right of the barns, Hyde, being some twenty feet ahead, looked over its top and saw several regiments of Confederates, jammed close together and waiting at the ready; so he gave the order left flank, and, still at the double quick, took his column past the barns and buildings toward an orchard on the hither side, hoping that he could get them back before they were cut off, for they were faced by ten times their number. By going through the orchard he expected to be able to take advantage of a hollow, and partially escape the destructive flank fire on his return.

To hope to keep the barns from which they had driven the sharpshooters was vain, for the single Maine regiment found itself opposed to portions of no less than four Confederate brigades, at least a dozen regiments all told. When the men got to the orchard fence, Sergeant Benson wrenched apart the tall pickets to let through Hyde's horse. While he was doing this, a shot struck his haversack, and the men all laughed at the sight of the flying hardtack.

Going into the orchard there was a rise of ground, and the Confederates fired several volleys at the Maine men, and then charged them. Hyde's horse was twice wounded, but was still able to go on.

No sooner were the men in blue beyond the fence than they got into line and met the Confederates, as they came crowding behind, with a slaughtering fire, and then charged, driving them back. The color corporal was still carrying the colors, though one of his arms had been broken; but when half way through the orchard, Hyde heard him call out as he fell, and turned back to save the colors, if possible.

The apple-trees were short and thick, and he could not see much, and the Confederates speedily got between him and his men. Immediately, with the cry of "Rally, boys, to save the Major," back surged the regiment, and a volley at arm's length again destroyed all the foremost of their pursuers; so they rescued both their commander and the flag, which was carried off by Corporal Ring.

Hyde then formed the regiment on the colors, sixty-eight men all told, out of two hundred and forty who had begun the charge, and they slowly marched back toward their place in the Union line, while the New Yorkers and Vermonters rose from the ground cheering and waving their hats.

Next day, when the Confederates had retired a little from the field, the color corporal, Campbell, was found in the orchard, dead, propped up against a tree, with his half-smoked pipe beside him.

THE DEATH
OF
STONEWALL
JACKSON

Like a servant of the Lord, with his bible and his sword,
Our general rode along us, to form us for the fight.

—MACAULAY.

THE DEATH OF
STONEWALL JACKSON

The Civil War has left, as all wars of brother against brother must leave, terrible and heartrending memories; but there remains as an offset the glory which has accrued to the nation by the countless deeds of heroism performed by both sides in the struggle. The captains and the armies that, after long years of dreary campaigning and bloody, stubborn fighting, brought the war to a close, have left us more than a reunited realm. North and South, all Americans, now have a common fund of glorious memories. We are the richer for each grim campaign, for each hard-fought battle. We are the richer for valor displayed alike by those who fought so valiantly for the right, and by those who, no less valiantly, fought for what they deemed the right. We have in us nobler capacities for what is great and good because of the infinite woe and suffering, and because of the splendid ultimate triumph. We hold that it was vital to the welfare, not only of our people on this continent, but of the whole human race, that the Union should be preserved and slavery abolished; that one flag should fly from the Great Lakes to the Rio Grande; that we should all be free in fact as well as in name, and that the United States should stand as one nation—the greatest nation on the earth. But we recognize gladly that, South as well as North, when the fight was once on, the leaders of the armies, and the soldiers whom they led, displayed the same qualities of daring and steadfast courage, of disinterested loyalty and enthusiasm, and of high devotion to an ideal.

The greatest general of the South was Lee, and his greatest lieutenant was Jackson. Both were Virginians, and both were strongly opposed to disunion. Lee went so far as to deny the right of secession, while Jackson insisted that the South ought to try to get its rights inside the Union, and not outside. But when Virginia joined the Southern Confederacy, and the war had actually begun, both men cast their lot with the South.

It is often said that the Civil War was in one sense a repetition of the old struggle between the Puritan and the Cavalier; but Puritan and Cavalier types were common to the two armies. In dash and light-hearted daring, Custer and Kearney stood as conspicuous as Stuart and Morgan; and, on the other hand, no Northern general approached the Roundhead type—the type of the stern, religious warriors who fought under Cromwell—so closely as Stonewall Jackson. He was a man of intense religious conviction, who carried into every thought and deed of his daily life the precepts of the faith he cherished. He was a tender and loving husband and father, kindhearted and gentle to all with whom he was brought in contact; yet in the times that tried men's souls, he proved not only a commander of genius, but a fighter of iron will and temper, who joyed in the battle, and always showed at his best when the danger was greatest. The vein of fanaticism that ran through his character helped to render him a terrible opponent. He knew no such word as falter, and when he had once put his hand to a piece of work, he did it thoroughly and with all his heart. It was quite in keeping with his character that this gentle, high-minded, and religious man should, early in the contest, have proposed to hoist the black flag, neither take nor give quarter, and make the war one of extermination. No such policy was practical in the nineteenth century and in the American Republic; but it would have seemed quite natural and proper to Jackson's ancestors, the grim Scotch-Irish, who defended Londonderry against the forces of the Stuart king, or to their forefathers, the Covenanters of Scotland, and the Puritans who in England rejoiced at the beheading of King Charles I.

In the first battle in which Jackson took part, the confused struggle at Bull Run, he gained his name of Stonewall from the firmness with which he kept his men to their work and repulsed the attack of the Union troops. From that time until his death, less than two years afterward, his career was one of brilliant and almost un-interrupted success; whether serving with an independent command in the Valley, or acting under Lee as his right arm in the pitched battles with McClellan, Pope, and

Burnside. Few generals as great as Lee have ever had as great a lieutenant as Jackson. He was a master of strategy and tactics, fearless of responsibility, able to instill into his men his own intense ardor in battle, and so quick in his movements, so ready to march as well as fight, that his troops were known to the rest of the army as the "foot cavalry."

In the spring of 1863 Hooker had command of the Army of the Potomac. Like McClellan, he was able to perfect the discipline of his forces and to organize them, and as a division commander he was better than McClellan, but he failed even more signally when given a great independent command. He had under him 120,000 men when, toward the end of April, he prepared to attack Lee's army, which was but half as strong.

The Union army lay opposite Fredericksburg, looking at the fortified heights where they had received so bloody a repulse at the beginning of the winter. Hooker decided to distract the attention of the Confederates by letting a small portion of his force, under General Sedgwick, attack Fredericksburg, while he himself took the bulk of the army across the river to the right hand so as to crush Lee by an assault on his flank.

All went well at the beginning, and on the first of May Hooker found himself at Chancellorsville, face-to-face with the bulk of Lee's forces; and Sedgwick, crossing the river and charging with the utmost determination, had driven out of Fredericksburg the Confederate division of Early; but when Hooker found himself in front of Lee he hesitated, faltered instead of pushing on, and allowed the consummate general to whom he was opposed to take the initiative.

Lee fully realized his danger, and saw that his only chance was, first to beat back Hooker, and then to turn and overwhelm Sedgwick, who was in his rear. He consulted with Jackson, and Jackson begged to be allowed to make one of his favorite flank attacks upon the Union army; attacks which could have been successfully delivered only by a skilled and resolute general, and by troops equally able to march and to fight. Lee consented, and Jackson at once made off. The country was thickly covered with a forest of rather small growth, for it was a wild region, in which there was still plenty of game. Shielded by the forest, Jackson marched his gray columns rapidly to the left along the narrow country roads until he was square on the flank of the Union right wing, which was held by the Eleventh Corps, under Howard. The Union scouts got track of the movement and reported it at headquarters, but the Union generals thought the Confederates were retreating; and when finally the scouts brought word to Howard that he was menaced by a flank attack he paid no heed to the information, and actually let his whole corps be surprised in broad daylight. Yet all the while the battle was going on elsewhere, and Berdan's sharpshooters had surrounded and captured a Georgia regiment, from which information was received showing definitely that Jackson was not retreating, and must be preparing to strike a heavy blow.

The Eleventh Corps had not the slightest idea that it was about to be assailed. The men were not even in line. Many of them had stacked their muskets and were lounging about, some playing cards, others cooking supper, intermingled with the pack-mules and beef cattle. While they were thus utterly unprepared Jackson's gray-clad veterans pushed straight through the forest and rushed fiercely to the attack. The first notice the troops of the Eleventh Corps received did not come from the pickets, but from the deer, rabbits and foxes which, fleeing from their coverts at the approach of the Confederates, suddenly came running over and into the Union lines. In another minute the frightened pickets came tumbling back, and right behind them came the long files of charging, yelling Confederates. With one fierce rush Jackson's men swept over the Union lines, and at a blow the Eleventh Corps became a horde of panicstruck fugitives. Some of the regiments resisted for a few moments, and then they too were carried away in the flight.

For a while it seemed as if the whole army would be swept off; but Hooker and his subordinates exerted every effort to restore order. It was imperative to gain time so that the untouched portions of the army could form across the line of the Confederate advance.

Keenan's regiment of Pennsylvania cavalry, but four hundred sabers strong, was accordingly sent full against the front of the ten thousand victorious Confederates.

Keenan himself fell, pierced by bayonets, and the charge was repulsed at once; but a few priceless moments had been saved, and Pleasanton had been given time to post twenty-two guns, loaded with double canister, where they would bear upon the enemy.

The Confederates advanced in a dense mass, yelling and cheering, and the discharge of the guns fairly blew them back across the works they had just taken. Again they charged, and again were driven back; and when the battle once more began the Union reinforcements had arrived.

It was about this time that Jackson himself was mortally wounded. He had been leading and urging on the advance of his men, cheering them with voice and gesture, his pale face flushed with joy and excitement, while from time to time as he sat on his horse he took off his hat and, looking upward, thanked heaven for the victory it had vouchsafed him.

As darkness drew near he was in the front, where friend and foe were mingled in almost inextricable confusion. He and his staff were fired at, at close range, by the Union troops, and, as they turned, were fired at again, through a mistake, by the Confederates behind them. Jackson fell, struck in several places. He was put in a litter and carried back; but he never lost consciousness, and when one of his generals complained of the terrible effect of the Union cannonade he answered:

"You must hold your ground."

For several days he lingered, hearing how Lee beat Hooker, in detail, and forced him back across the river. Then the old Puritan died. At the end his mind wandered, and he thought he was again commanding in battle, and his last words were:

"Let us cross over the river and rest in the shade."

Thus perished Stonewall Jackson, one of the ablest of soldiers and one of the most upright of men, in the last of his many triumphs.

THE CHARGE
AT GETTYSBURG

For the Lord
  On the whirlwind is abroad;
In the earthquake he has spoken;
  He has smitten with his thunder
  The iron walls asunder,
And the gates of brass are broken!

                    —WHITTIER.

With bray of the trumpet,
  And roll of the drum,
And keen ring of bugle
  The cavalry come:
Sharp clank the steel scabbards,
  The bridle-chains ring,
And foam from red nostrils
  The wild chargers fling!

Tramp, tramp o'er the greensward
  That quivers below,
Scarce held by the curb bit
  The fierce horses go!
And the grim-visaged colonel,
  With ear-rending shout,
Peals forth to the squadrons
  The order, "Trot Out"!

                —FRANCIS A. DURIVAGE.

THE CHARGE AT GETTYSBURG

The battle of Chancellorsville marked the zenith of Confederate good fortune. Immediately afterward, in June, 1863, Lee led the victorious army of Northern Virginia into Pennsylvania. The South was now the invader, not the invaded, and its heart beat proudly with hopes of success; but these hopes went down in bloody wreck on July 4, when word was sent to the world that the high valor of Virginia had failed at last on the field of Gettysburg, and that in the far West Vicksburg had been taken by the army of the "silent soldier."

At Gettysburg Lee had under him some seventy thousand men, and his opponent, Meade, about ninety thousand. Both armies were composed mainly of seasoned veterans, trained to the highest point by campaign after campaign and battle after battle; and there was nothing to choose between them as to the fighting power of the rank and file. The Union army was the larger, yet most of the time it stood on the defensive; for the difference between the generals, Lee and Meade, was greater than could be bridged by twenty thousand men. For three days the battle raged. No other battle of recent time has been so obstinate and so bloody. The victorious Union army lost a greater percentage in killed and wounded than the allied armies of England, Germany, and the Netherlands lost at Waterloo. Four of its seven corps suffered each a greater relative loss than befell the world-renowned British infantry on the day that saw the doom of the French emperor. The defeated Confederates at Gettysburg lost, relatively, as many men as the defeated French at Waterloo; but whereas the French army became a mere rabble, Lee withdrew his formidable soldiery with their courage unbroken, and their fighting power only diminished by their actual losses in the field.

The decisive moment of the battle, and perhaps of the whole war, was in the afternoon of the third day, when Lee sent forward his choicest troops in a last effort to break the middle of the Union line. The center of the attacking force was Pickett's division, the flower of the Virginia infantry; but many other brigades took part in the assault, and the column, all told, numbered over fifteen thousand men. At the same time, the Confederates attacked the Union left to create a diversion.

The attack was preceded by a terrific cannonade, Lee gathering one hundred and fifteen guns, and opening a fire on the center of the Union line. In response, Hunt, the Union chief of artillery, and Tyler, of the artillery reserves, gathered eighty guns on the crest of the gently sloping hill, where attack was threatened. For two hours, from one till three, the cannonade lasted, and the batteries on both sides suffered severely. In both the Union and Confederate lines caissons were blown up by the fire, riderless horses dashed hither and thither, the dead lay in heaps, and throngs of wounded streamed to the rear. Every man lay down and sought what cover he could. It was evident that the Confederate cannonade was but a prelude to a great infantry attack, and at three o'clock Hunt ordered the fire to stop, that the guns might cool, to be ready for the coming assault. The Confederates thought that they had silenced the hostile artillery, and for a few minutes their firing continued; then, suddenly, it ceased, and there was a lull.

The men on the Union side who were not at the point directly menaced peered anxiously across the space between the lines to watch the next move, while the men in the divisions which it was certain were about to be assaulted, lay hugging the ground and gripping their muskets, excited, but confident and resolute. They saw the smoke clouds rise slowly from the opposite crest, where the Confederate army lay, and the sunlight glinted again on the long line of brass and iron guns which had been hidden from view during the cannonade. In another moment, out of the lifting smoke there appeared, beautiful and terrible, the picked thousands of the Southern army coming on to the assault. They advanced in three lines, each over a mile long, and in perfect order. Pickett's Virginians held the center, with on their left the North Carolinians of Pender and Pettigrew, and on their right the Alabama regiments of Wilcox; and there were also Georgian and Tennessee regiments in the attacking force. Pickett's division, however, was the only one able to press its charge home. After leaving the woods where they started, the Confederates had nearly a mile and a half to go in their charge. As the Virginians moved, they bent slightly to the left, so as to leave a gap between them and the Alabamians on the right.

The Confederate lines came on magnificently. As they crossed the Emmetsburg Pike the eighty guns on the Union crest, now cool and in good shape, opened upon them, first with shot and then with shell. Great gaps were made every second in the ranks, but the gray-clad soldiers closed up to the center, and the color-bearers leaped to the front, shaking and waving the flags. The Union infantry reserved their fire until the Confederates were within easy range, when the musketry crashed out with a roar, and the big guns began to fire grape and canister. On came the Confederates, the men falling by hundreds, the colors fluttering in front like a little forest; for as fast as a color-bearer was shot some one else seized the flag from his hand before it fell. The North Carolinians were more exposed to the fire than any other portion of the attacking force, and they were broken before they reached the line.

There was a gap between the Virginians and the Alabama troops, and this was taken advantage of by Stannard's Vermont brigade and a demi-brigade under Gates, of the 20th New York, who were thrust forward into it.

Stannard changed front with his regiments and fell on Pickett's forces in flank, and Gates continued the attack. When thus struck in the flank, the Virginians could not defend themselves, and they crowded off toward the center to avoid the pressure. Many of them were killed or captured; many were driven back; but two of the brigades, headed by General Armistead, forced their way forward to the stone wall on the crest, where the Pennsylvania regiments were posted under Gibbon and Webb.

The Union guns fired to the last moment, until of the two batteries immediately in front of the charging Virginians every officer but one had been struck. One of the mortally wounded officers was young Cushing, a brother of the hero of the Albemarle fight. He was almost cut in two, but holding his body together with one hand, with the other he fired his last gun, and fell dead, just as Armistead, pressing forward at the head of his men, leaped the wall, waving his hat on his sword. Immediately afterward the battle-flags of the foremost Confederate regiments crowned the crest; but their strength was spent. The Union troops moved forward with the bayonet, and the remnant of Pickett's division, attacked on all sides, either surrendered or retreated down the hill again. Armistead fell, dying, by the body of the dead Cushing. Both Gibbon and Webb were wounded. Of Pickett's command two thirds were killed, wounded or captured, and every brigade commander and every field officer, save one, fell. The Virginians tried to rally, but were broken and driven again by Gates, while Stannard repeated, at the expense of the Alabamians, the movement he had made against the Virginians, and, reversing his front, attacked them in flank. Their lines were torn by the batteries in front, and they fell back before the Vermonters' attack, and Stannard reaped a rich harvest of prisoners and of battle-flags.

The charge was over. It was the greatest charge in any battle of modern times, and it had failed. It would be impossible to surpass the gallantry of those that made it, or the gallantry of those that withstood it. Had there been in command of the Union army a general like Grant, it would have been followed by a counter-charge, and in all probability the war would have been shortened by nearly two years; but no countercharge was made.

As the afternoon waned, a fierce cavalry fight took place on the Union right. Stuart, the famous Confederate cavalry commander, had moved forward to turn the Union right, but he was met by Gregg's cavalry, and there followed a contest, at close quarters, with "the white arm." It closed with a desperate melee, in which the Confederates, charged under Generals Wade Hampton and Fitz Lee, were met in mid career by the Union Generals Custer and McIntosh. All four fought, saber in hand, at the head of their troopers, and every man on each side was put into the struggle. Custer, his yellow hair flowing, his face aflame with the eager joy of battle, was in the thick of the fight, rising in his stirrups as he called to his famous Michigan swordsmen: "Come on, you Wolverines, come on!" All that the Union infantry, watching eagerly from their lines, could see, was a vast dust-cloud where flakes of light shimmered as the sun shone upon the swinging sabers. At last the

Confederate horsemen were beaten back, and they did not come forward again or seek to renew the combat; for Pickett's charge had failed, and there was no longer hope of Confederate victory.

When night fell, the Union flags waved in triumph on the field of Gettysburg; but over thirty thousand men lay dead or wounded, strewn through wood and meadow, on field and hill, where the three days' fight had surged.

GENERAL GRANT AND THE VICKSBURG CAMPAIGN

What flag is this you carry
    Along the sea and shore?
The same our grandsires lifted up—
    The same our fathers bore.
In many a battle's tempest
    It shed the crimson rain—
What God has woven in his loom
    Let no man rend in twain.
To Canaan, to Canaan,
    The Lord has led us forth,
To plant upon the rebel towers
    The banners of the North.

                            —HOLMES.

GENERAL GRANT AND THE VICKSBURG CAMPAIGN

On January 29, 1863, General Grant took command of the army intended to operate against Vicksburg, the last place held by the rebels on the Mississippi, and the only point at which they could cross the river and keep up communication with their armies and territory in the southwest.

It was the first high ground below Memphis, was very strongly fortified, and was held by a large army under General Pemberton. The complete possession of the Mississippi was absolutely essential to the National Government, because the control of that great river would cut the Confederacy in two, and do more, probably, than anything else, to make the overthrow of the Rebellion both speedy and certain.

The natural way to invest and capture so strong a place, defended and fortified as Vicksburg was, would have been, if the axioms of the art of war had been adhered to, by a system of gradual approaches. A strong base should have been established at Memphis, and then the army and the fleet moved gradually forward, building storehouses and taking strong positions as they went.

To do this, however, it first would have been necessary to withdraw the army from the positions it then held not far above Vicksburg, on the western bank of the river. But such a movement, at that time, would not have been understood by the country, and would have had a discouraging effect on the public mind, which it was most essential to avoid. The elections of 1862 had gone against the government, and there was great discouragement throughout the North.

Voluntary enlistments had fallen off, a draft had been ordered, and the peace party was apparently gaining rapidly in strength. General Grant, looking at this grave political situation with the eye of a statesman, decided, as a soldier, that under no circumstances would he withdraw the army, but that, whatever happened, he would "press forward to a decisive victory." In this determination he never faltered, but drove straight at his object until, five months later, the great Mississippi stronghold fell before him.

Efforts were made through the winter to reach Vicksburg from the north by cutting canals, and by attempts to get in through the bayous and tributary streams of the great river. All these expedients failed, however, one after another, as Grant, from the beginning, had feared that they would. He, therefore, took another and widely different line, and determined to cross the river from the western to the eastern bank below Vicksburg, to the south. With the aid of the fleet, which ran the batteries successfully, he moved his army down the west bank until he reached a point beyond the possibility of attack, while a diversion by Sherman at Haines' Bluff, above Vicksburg, kept Pemberton in his fortifications. On April 26, Grant began to move his men over the river and landed them at Bruinsburg. "When this was effected," he writes, "I felt a degree of relief scarcely ever equaled since. Vicksburg was not yet taken, it is true, nor were its defenders demoralized by any of our previous movements. I was now in the enemy's country, with a vast river and the stronghold of Vicksburg between me and my base of supplies, but I was on dry ground, on the same side of the river with the enemy."

The situation was this: The enemy had about sixty thousand men at Vicksburg, Haines' Bluff, and at Jackson, Mississippi, about fifty miles east of Vicksburg. Grant, when he started, had about thirty-three thousand men. It was absolutely necessary for success that Grant, with inferior numbers, should succeed in destroying the smaller forces to the eastward, and thus prevent their union with Pemberton and the main army at Vicksburg. His plan, in brief; was to fight and defeat a superior enemy separately and in detail. He lost no time in putting his plan into action, and pressing forward quickly, met a detachment of the enemy at Port Gibson and defeated them. Thence he marched to Grand Gulf, on the Mississippi, which he took, and which he had planned to make a base of supply. When he reached Grand Gulf, however, he found that he would be obliged to wait a month, in order to obtain the reinforcements which he expected from

General Banks at Port Hudson. He, therefore, gave up the idea of making Grand Gulf a base, and Sherman having now joined him with his corps, Grant struck at once into the interior. He took nothing with him except ammunition, and his army was in the lightest marching order. This enabled him to move with great rapidity, but deprived him of his wagon trains, and of all munitions of war except cartridges. Everything, however, in this campaign, depended on quickness, and Grant's decision, as well as all his movements, marked the genius of the great soldier, which consists very largely in knowing just when to abandon the accepted military axioms.

Pressing forward, Grant met the enemy, numbering between seven and eight thousand, at Raymond, and readily defeated them. He then marched on toward Jackson, fighting another action at Clinton, and at Jackson he struck General Joseph Johnston, who had arrived at that point to take command of all the rebel forces. Johnston had with him, at the moment, about eleven thousand men, and stood his ground. There was a sharp fight, but Grant easily defeated the enemy, and took possession of the town. This was an important point, for Jackson was the capital of the State of Mississippi, and was a base of military supplies. Grant destroyed the factories and the munitions of war which were gathered there, and also came into possession of the line of railroad which ran from Jackson to Vicksburg. While he was thus engaged, an intercepted message revealed to him the fact that Pemberton, in accordance with Johnston's orders, had come out of Vicksburg with twenty-five thousand men, and was moving eastward against him. Pemberton, however, instead of holding a straight line against Grant, turned at first to the south, with the view of breaking the latter's line of communication. This was not a success, for, as Grant says, with grim humor, "I had no line of communication to break"; and, moreover, it delayed Pemberton when delay was of value to Grant in finishing Johnston. After this useless turn to the southward Pemberton resumed his march to the east, as he should have done in the beginning, in accordance with Johnston's orders; but Grant was now more than ready. He did not wait the coming of Pemberton.

Leaving Jackson as soon as he heard of the enemy's advance from Vicksburg, he marched rapidly westward and struck Pemberton at Champion Hills. The forces were at this time very nearly matched, and the severest battle of the campaign ensued, lasting four hours. Grant, however, defeated Pemberton completely, and came very near capturing his entire force. With a broken army, Pemberton fell back on Vicksburg.

Grant pursued without a moment's delay, and came up with the rear guard at Big Black River. A sharp engagement followed, and the Confederates were again defeated. Grant then crossed the Big Black and the next day was before Vicksburg, with his enemy inside the works.

When Grant crossed the Mississippi at Bruinsburg and struck into the interior, he, of course, passed out of communication with Washington, and he did not hear from there again until May 11, when, just as his troops were engaging in the battle of Black River Bridge, an officer appeared from Port Hudson with an order from General Halleck to return to Grand Gulf and thence cooperate with Banks against Port Hudson.

Grant replied that the order came too late. "The bearer of the dispatch insisted that I ought to obey the order, and was giving arguments to support the position, when I heard a great cheering to the right of our line, and looking in that direction, saw Lawler, in his shirt-sleeves, leading a charge on the enemy. I immediately mounted my horse and rode in the direction of the charge, and saw no more of the officer who had delivered the message; I think not even to this day." When Grant reached Vicksburg, there was no further talk of recalling him to Grand Gulf or Port Hudson. The authorities at Washington then saw plainly enough what had been done in the interior of Mississippi, far from the reach of telegraphs or mail.

As soon as the National troops reached Vicksburg an assault was attempted, but the place was too strong, and the attack was repulsed, with heavy loss. Grant then settled down to a siege, and Lincoln and Halleck now sent him ample reinforcements. He no longer needed to ask for them. His campaign had explained itself, and in a short time he had seventy thousand men under his command. His lines were soon made so strong that it was impossible for the defenders of Vicksburg to break through them, and although Johnston had gathered troops again to the eastward, an assault from that quarter on the National army, now so largely reinforced, was practically out of the question. Tighter and tighter Grant drew his lines about the city, where, every day, the suffering became more intense. It is not necessary to give the details of the siege. On July 4, 1863, Vicksburg surrendered, the Mississippi was in control of the National forces from its source to its mouth, and the Confederacy was rent in twain. On the same day Lee was beaten at Gettysburg, and these two great victories really crushed the Rebellion, although much hard fighting remained to be done before the end was reached.

Grant's campaign against Vicksburg deserves to be compared with that of Napoleon which resulted in the fall of Ulm. It was the most brilliant single campaign of the war. With an inferior force, and abandoning his lines of communication, moving with a marvelous rapidity through a difficult country, Grant struck the superior forces of the enemy on the line from Jackson to Vicksburg. He crushed Johnston before Pemberton could get to him, and he flung Pemberton back into Vicksburg before Johnston could rally from the defeat which had been inflicted. With an inferior force, Grant was superior at every point of contest, and he won every fight. Measured by the skill displayed and the result achieved, there is no campaign in our history which better deserves study and admiration.

ROBERT GOULD SHAW

Brave, good, and true,
I see him stand before me now,
And read again on that young brow,
Where every hope was new,
HOW SWEET WERE LIFE! Yet, by the mouth firm-set,
And look made up for Duty's utmost debt,
I could divine he knew
That death within the sulphurous hostile lines,
In the mere wreck of nobly-pitched designs,
Plucks hearts-ease, and not rue.

Right in the van,
On the red ramparts slippery swell,
With heart that beat a charge, he fell,
Foeward, as fits a man;
But the high soul burns on to light men's feet
Where death for noble ends makes dying sweet;
His life her crescent's span
Orbs full with share in their undarkening days
Who ever climbed the battailous steeps of praise
Since valor's praise began.

We bide our chance,
Unhappy, and make terms with Fate
A little more to let us wait;
He leads for aye the advance,
Hope's forlorn-hopes that plant the desperate good
For nobler Earths and days of manlier mood;
Our wall of circumstance
Cleared at a bound, he flashes o'er the fight,
A saintly shape of fame, to cheer the right
And steel each wavering glance.

I write of one,
While with dim eyes I think of three;
Who weeps not others fair and brave as he?
Ah, when the fight is won,
Dear Land, whom triflers now make bold to scorn
(Thee from whose forehead Earth awaits her morn),
How nobler shall the sun
Flame in thy sky, how braver breathe thy air,
That thou bred'st children who for thee could dare
And die as thine have done.

                                        —LOWELL.

ROBERT GOULD SHAW

Robert Gould Shaw was born in Boston on October 10, 1837, the son of Francis and Sarah Sturgis Shaw. When he was about nine years old, his parents moved to Staten Island, and he was educated there, and at school in the neighborhood of New York, until he went to Europe in 1853, where he remained traveling and studying for the next three years. He entered Harvard College in 1856, and left at the end of his third year, in order to accept an advantageous business offer in New York.

Even as a boy he took much interest in politics, and especially in the question of slavery. He voted for Lincoln in 1860, and at that time enlisted as a private in the New York 7th Regiment, feeling that there was likelihood of trouble, and that there would be a demand for soldiers to defend the country. His foresight was justified only too soon, and on April 19, 1861, he marched with his regiment to Washington. The call for the 7th Regiment was only for thirty days, and at the expiration of that service he applied for and obtained a commission as second lieutenant in the 2nd Massachusetts, and left with that regiment for Virginia in July, 1861. He threw himself eagerly into his new duties, and soon gained a good position in the regiment. At Cedar Mountain he was an aid on General Gordon's staff, and was greatly exposed in the performance of his duties during the action. He was also with his regiment at Antietam, and was in the midst of the heavy fighting of that great battle.

Early in 1863, the Government determined to form negro regiments, and Governor Andrew offered Shaw, who had now risen to the rank of captain, the colonelcy of one to be raised in Massachusetts, the first black regiment recruited under State authority. It was a great compliment to receive this offer, but Shaw hesitated as to his capacity for such a responsible post. He first wrote a letter declining, on the ground that he did not feel that he had ability enough for the undertaking, and then changed his mind, and telegraphed Governor Andrew that he would accept.

It is not easy to realize it now, but his action then in accepting this command required high moral courage, of a kind quite different from that which he had displayed already on the field of battle. The prejudice against the blacks was still strong even in the North. There was a great deal of feeling among certain classes against enlisting black regiments at all, and the officers who undertook to recruit and lead negroes were exposed to much attack and criticism. Shaw felt, however, that this very opposition made it all the more incumbent on him to undertake the duty.

He wrote on February 8:

After I have undertaken this work, I shall feel that what I have to do is to prove that the negro can be made a good soldier. . . . I am inclined to think that the undertaking will not meet with so much opposition as was at first supposed. All sensible men in the army, of all parties, after a little thought, say that it is the best thing that can be done, and surely those at home who are not brave or patriotic enough to enlist should not ridicule or throw obstacles in the way of men who are going to fight for them. There is a great prejudice against it, but now that it has become a government matter, that will probably wear away. At any rate I sha'n't be frightened out of it by its unpopularity. I feel convinced I shall never regret having taken this step, as far as I myself am concerned; for while I was undecided, I felt ashamed of myself as if I were cowardly.

Colonel Shaw went at once to Boston, after accepting his new duty, and began the work of raising and drilling the 54th Regiment. He met with great success, for he and his officers labored heart and soul, and the regiment repaid their efforts. On March 30, he wrote: "The mustering officer who was here to-day is a Virginian, and has always thought it was a great joke to try to make soldiers of 'niggers,' but he tells me now that he has never mustered in so fine a set of men, though about twenty thousand had passed through his hands since September."

On May 28, Colonel Shaw left Boston, and his march through the city was a triumph. The appearance of his regiment made a profound impression, and was one of the events of the war which those who saw it never forgot.

The regiment was ordered to South Carolina, and when they were off Cape Hatteras, Colonel Shaw wrote:

> The more I think of the passage of the 54th through Boston, the more wonderful it seems to me just remember our own doubts and fears, and other people's sneering and pitying remarks when we began last winter, and then look at the perfect triumph of last Thursday. We have gone quietly along, forming the first regiment, and at last left Boston amidst greater enthusiasm than has been seen since the first three months' troops left for the war. Truly, I ought to be thankful for all my happiness and my success in life so far; and if the raising of colored troops prove such a benefit to the country and to the blacks as many people think it will, I shall thank God a thousand times that I was led to take my share in it.

He had, indeed, taken his share in striking one of the most fatal blows to the barbarism of slavery which had yet been struck. The formation of the black regiments did more for the emancipation of the negro and the recognition of his rights, than almost anything else. It was impossible, after that, to say that men who fought and gave their lives for the Union and for their own freedom were not entitled to be free. The acceptance of the command of a black regiment by such men as Shaw and his fellow-officers was the great act which made all this possible.

After reaching South Carolina, Colonel Shaw was with his regiment at Port Royal and on the islands of that coast for rather more than a month, and on July 18 he was offered the post of honor in an assault upon Fort Wagner, which was ordered for that night. He had proved that the negroes could be made into a good regiment, and now the second great opportunity had come, to prove their fighting quality. He wanted to demonstrate that his men could fight side by side with white soldiers, and show to somebody beside their officers what stuff they were made of.

He, therefore, accepted the dangerous duty with gladness. Late in the day the troops were marched across Folly and Morris islands and formed in line of battle within six hundred yards of Fort Wagner. At half-past seven the order for the charge was given, and the regiment advanced.

When they were within a hundred yards of the fort, the rebel fire opened with such effect that the first battalion hesitated and wavered. Colonel Shaw sprang to the front, and waving his sword, shouted: "Forward, 54th!" With another cheer, the men rushed through the ditch, and gained a parapet on the right. Colonel Shaw was one of the first to scale the walls. As he stood erect, a noble figure, ordering his men forward and shouting to them to press on, he was shot dead and fell into the fort.

After his fall, the assault was repulsed.

General Haywood, commanding the rebel forces, said to a Union prisoner:

> I knew Colonel Shaw before the war, and then esteemed him. Had he been in command of white troops, I should have given him an honorable burial.
>
> As it is, I shall bury him in the common trench, with the negroes that fell with him.

He little knew that he was giving the dead soldier the most honorable burial that man could have devised, for the savage words told unmistakably that Robert Shaw's work had not been in vain. The order to bury him with his "niggers," which ran through the North and remained fixed in our history, showed, in a flash of light, the hideous barbarism of a system which made such things and such feelings possible.

It also showed that slavery was wounded to the death, and that the brutal phrase was the angry snarl of a dying tiger. Such words rank with the action of Charles Stuart, when he had the bones of Oliver Cromwell and Robert Blake torn from their graves and flung on dunghills or fixed on Temple Bar.

Robert Shaw fell in battle at the head of his men, giving his life to his country, as did many another gallant man during those four years of conflict. But he did something more than this. He faced prejudice and hostility in the North, and confronted the blind and savage rage of the South, in order to demonstrate to the world that the human beings who were held in bondage could vindicate their right to freedom by fighting and dying for it. He helped mightily in the great task of destroying human slavery, and in uplifting an oppressed and down-trodden race. He brought to this work the qualities which were particularly essential for his success. He had all that birth and wealth, breeding, education, and tradition could give. He offered up, in full measure, all those things which make life most worth living. He was handsome and beloved. He had a serene and beautiful nature, and was at once brave and simple. Above all things, he was fitted for the task which he performed and for the sacrifice which he made. The call of the country and of the time came to him, and he was ready. He has been singled out for remembrance from among many others of equal sacrifice, and a monument is rising to his memory in Boston, because it was his peculiar fortune to live and die for a great principle of humanity, and to stand forth as an ideal and beautiful figure in a struggle where the onward march of civilization was at stake. He lived in those few and crowded years a heroic life, and he met a heroic death. When he fell, sword in hand, on the parapet of Wagner, leading his black troops in a desperate assault, we can only say of him as Bunyan said of "Valiant for Truth": "And then he passed over, and all the trumpets sounded for him on the other side."

CHARLES RUSSELL LOWELL

Wut's wurds to them whose faith an' truth
    On war's red techstone rang true metal,
Who ventered life an' love an, youth
    For the gret prize o' death in battle?
To him who, deadly hurt, agen
    Flashed on afore the charge's thunder,
Tippin' with fire the bolt of men
    Thet rived the rebel line asunder?

                    —LOWELL.

CHARLES RUSSELL LOWELL

Charles Russell Lowell was born in Boston, January 2, 1835. He was the eldest son of Charles Russell and Anna Cabot (Jackson) Lowell, and the nephew of James Russell Lowell. He bore the name, distinguished in many branches, of a family which was of the best New England stock. Educated in the Boston public schools, he entered Harvard College in 1850.

Although one of the youngest members of his class, he went rapidly to the front, and graduated not only the first scholar of his year, but the foremost man of his class. He was, however, much more than a fine scholar, for even then he showed unusual intellectual qualities. He read widely and loved letters. He was a student of philosophy and religion, a thinker, and, best of all, a man of ideals—"the glory of youth," as he called them in his valedictory oration. But he was something still better and finer than a mere idealist; he was a man of action, eager to put his ideals into practice and bring them to the test of daily life.

With his mind full of plans for raising the condition of workingmen while he made his own career, he entered the iron mills of the Ames Company, at Chicopee. Here he remained as a workingman for six months, and then received an important post in the Trenton Iron Works of New Jersey. There his health broke down. Consumption threatened him, and all his bright hopes and ambitions were overcast and checked. He was obliged to leave his business and go to Europe, where he traveled for two years, fighting the dread disease that was upon him. In 1858 he returned, and took a position on a Western railroad. Although the work was new to him, he manifested the same capacity that he had always shown, and more especially his power over other men and his ability in organization. In two years his health was reestablished, and in 1860 he took charge of the Mount Savage Iron Works, at Cumberland, Maryland. He was there when news came of the attack made by the mob upon the 6th Massachusetts Regiment, in Baltimore. Two days later he had made his way to Washington, one of the first comers from the North, and at once applied for a commission in the regular army. While he was waiting, he employed himself in looking after the Massachusetts troops, and also, it is understood, as a scout for the Government, dangerous work which suited his bold and adventurous nature.

In May he received his commission as captain in the United States cavalry. Employed at first in recruiting and then in drill, he gave himself up to the study of tactics and the science of war. The career above all others to which he was suited had come to him. The field, at last, lay open before him, where all his great qualities of mind and heart, his high courage, his power of leadership and of organization, and his intellectual powers could find full play. He moved rapidly forward, just as he had already done in college and in business. His regiment, in 1862, was under Stoneman in the Peninsula, and was engaged in many actions, where Lowell's cool bravery made him constantly conspicuous.

At the close of the campaign he was brevetted major, for distinguished services at Williamsburg and Slatersville.

In July, Lowell was detailed for duty as an aid to General McClellan.

At Malvern Hill and South Mountain his gallantry and efficiency were strongly shown, but it was at Antietam that he distinguished himself most. Sent with orders to General Sedgwick's division, he found it retreating in confusion, under a hot fire. He did not stop to think of orders, but rode rapidly from point to point of the line, rallying company after company by the mere force and power of his word and look, checking the rout, while the storm of bullets swept all round him. His horse was shot under him, a ball passed through his coat, another broke his sword-hilt, but he came off unscathed, and his service was recognized by his being sent to Washington with the captured flags of the enemy.

The following winter he was ordered to Boston, to recruit a regiment of cavalry, of which he was appointed colonel. While the recruiting was going on, a serious mutiny broke out, but the man who, like Cromwell's soldiers, "rejoiced greatly" in the day of battle was entirely capable of meeting this different trial. He shot the ringleader dead, and by the force of his own strong will quelled the outbreak completely and at once.

In May, he went to Virginia with his regiment, where he was engaged in resisting and following Mosby, and the following summer he was opposed to General Early in the neighborhood of Washington. On July 14, when on a reconnoissance his advance guard was surprised, and he met them retreating in wild confusion, with the enemy at their heels. Riding into the midst of the fugitives, Lowell shouted, "Dismount!" The sharp word of command, the presence of the man himself, and the magic of discipline prevailed. The men sprang down, drew up in line, received the enemy, with a heavy fire, and as the assailants wavered, Lowell advanced at once, and saved the day.

In July, he was put in command of the "Provisional Brigade," and joined the army of the Shenandoah, of which in August General Sheridan took command. He was so struck with Lowell's work during the next month that in September he put him in command of the "Reserved Brigade," a very fine body of cavalry and artillery. In the fierce and continuous fighting that ensued Lowell was everywhere conspicuous, and in thirteen weeks he had as many horses shot under him. But he now had scope to show more than the dashing gallantry which distinguished him always and everywhere. His genuine military ability, which surely would have led him to the front rank of soldiers had his life been spared, his knowledge, vigilance, and nerve all now became apparent. One brilliant action succeeded another, but the end was drawing near. It came at last on the famous day of Cedar Creek, when Sheridan rode down from Winchester and saved the battle. Lowell had advanced early in the morning on the right, and his attack prevented the disaster on that wing which fell upon the surprised army. He then moved to cover the retreat, and around to the extreme left, where he held his position near Middletown against repeated assaults. Early in the day his last horse was shot under him, and a little later, in a charge at one o'clock, he was struck in the right breast by a spent ball, which embedded itself in the muscles of the chest. Voice and strength left him. "It is only my poor lung," he announced, as they urged him to go to the rear; "you would not have me leave the field without having shed blood." As a matter of fact, the "poor" lung had collapsed, and there was an internal hemorrhage. He lay thus, under a rude shelter, for an hour and a half, and then came the order to advance along the whole line, the victorious advance of Sheridan and the rallied army. Lowell was helped to his saddle. "I feel well now," he whispered, and, giving his orders through one of his staff, had his brigade ready first. Leading the great charge, he dashed forward, and, just when the fight was hottest, a sudden cry went up: "The colonel is hit!" He fell from the saddle, struck in the neck by a ball which severed the spine, and was borne by his officers to a house in the village, where, clear in mind and calm in spirit, he died a few hours afterward.

"I do not think there was a quality," said General

Sheridan, "which I could have added to Lowell. He was the perfection of a man and a soldier." On October 19, the very day on which he fell, his commission was signed to be a brigadier-general.

This was a noble life and a noble death, worthy of much thought and admiration from all men. Yet this is not all. It is well for us to see how such a man looked upon what he was doing, and what it meant to him.

Lowell was one of the silent heroes so much commended by Carlyle. He never wrote of himself or his own exploits. As some one well said, he had "the impersonality of genius." But in a few remarkable passages in his private letters, we can see how the meaning of life and of that great time unrolled itself before his inner eyes. In June, 1861, he wrote:

I cannot say I take any great pleasure in the contemplation of the future. I fancy you feel much as I do about the profitableness of a soldier's life, and would not think of trying it, were it not for a muddled and twisted idea that somehow or other this fight was going to be one in which decent men ought to engage for the sake of humanity,—I use the word in its ordinary sense. It seems to me that within a year the slavery question will again take a prominent place, and that many cases will arise in which we may get fearfully in the wrong if we put our cause wholly in the hands of fighting men and foreign legions.

In June, 1863, he wrote:

I wonder whether my theories about self-culture, etc., would ever have been modified so much, whether I should ever have seen what a necessary failure they lead to, had it not been for this war. Now I feel every day, more and more, that a man has no right to himself at all; that, indeed, he can do nothing useful unless he recognizes this clearly. Here again, on July 3, is a sentence which it is well to take to heart, and for all men to remember when their ears are deafened with the cry that war, no matter what the cause, is the worst thing possible, because it interferes with comfort, trade, and money-making: "Wars are bad," Lowell writes, "but there are many things far worse. Anything immediately comfortable in our affairs I don't see; but comfortable times are not the ones that make a nation great."

On July 24, he says:

Many nations fail, that one may become great; ours will fail, unless we gird up our loins and do humble and honest days' work, without trying to do the thing by the job, or to get a great nation made by a patent process. It is not safe to say that we shall not have victories till we are ready for them. We shall have victories, and whether or no we are ready for them depends upon ourselves; if we are not ready, we shall fail,—voila tout. If you ask, what if we do fail? I have nothing to say; I shouldn't cry over a nation or two, more or less, gone under.

Finally, on September 10, a little more than a month before his death, he wrote to a disabled officer:

I hope that you are going to live like a plain republican, mindful of the beauty and of the duty of simplicity. Nothing fancy now, sir, if you please; it's disreputable to spend money when the government is so hard up, and when there are so many poor officers. I hope that you have outgrown all foolish ambitions, and are now content to become a "useful citizen." Don't grow rich; if you once begin, you will find it much more difficult to be a useful citizen. Don't seek office, but don't "disremember" that the "useful citizen" always holds his time, his trouble, his money, and his life ready at the hint of his country. The useful citizen is a mighty, unpretending hero; but we are not going to have any country very long, unless such heroism is developed. There, what a stale sermon I'm preaching. But, being a soldier, it does seem to me that I should like nothing so well as being a useful citizen. Well, trying to be one, I mean. I shall stay in the service, of course, till the war is over, or till I'm disabled; but then I look forward to a pleasanter career.

I believe I have lost all my ambitions. I don't think

I would turn my hand to be a distinguished chemist or a famous mathematician. All I now care about is to be a useful citizen, with money enough to buy bread and firewood, and to teach my children to ride on horseback, and look strangers in the face, especially Southern strangers.

There are profound and lofty lessons of patriotism and conduct in these passages, and a very noble philosophy of life and duty both as a man and as a citizen of a great republic. They throw a flood of light on the great underlying forces which enabled the American people to save themselves in that time of storm and stress. They are the utterances of a very young man, not thirty years old when he died in battle, but much beyond thirty in head and heart, tried and taught as he had been in a great war. What precisely such young men thought they were fighting for is put strikingly by Lowell's younger brother James, who was killed at Glendale, July 4, 1862. In 1861, James Lowell wrote to his classmates, who had given him a sword:

Those who died for the cause, not of the Constitution and the laws,—a superficial cause, the rebels have now the same,—but of civilization and law, and the self-restrained freedom which is their result. As the Greeks at Marathon and Salamis, Charles Martel and the Franks at Tours, and the Germans at the Danube, saved Europe from Asiatic barbarism, so we, at places to be famous in future times, shall have saved America from a similar tide of barbarism; and we may hope to be purified and strengthened ourselves by the struggle.

This is a remarkable passage and a deep thought. Coming from a young fellow of twenty-four, it is amazing. But the fiery trial of the times taught fiercely and fast, and James Lowell, just out of college, could see in the red light around him that not merely the freedom of a race and the saving of a nation were at stake, but that behind all this was the forward movement of civilization, brought once again to the arbitrament of the sword. Slavery was barbarous and barbarizing. It had dragged down the civilization of the South to a level from which it would take generations to rise up again. Was this barbarous force now to prevail in the United States in the nineteenth century? Was it to destroy a great nation, and fetter human progress in the New World? That was the great question back of, beyond and above all. Should this force of barbarism sweep conquering over the land, wrecking an empire in its onward march, or should it be flung back as Miltiades flung back Asia at Marathon, and Charles Martel stayed the coming of Islam at Tours? The brilliant career, the shining courage, best seen always where the dead were lying thickest, the heroic death of Charles Lowell, are good for us all to know and to remember. Yet this imperfect story of his life has not been placed here for these things alone. Many thousand others, officers and soldiers alike, in the great Civil War gave their lives as freely as he, and brought to the service of their country the best that was in them. He was a fine example of many who, like him, offered up all they had for their country. But Lowell was also something more than this. He was a high type of a class, and a proof of certain very important things, and this is a point worthy of much consideration.

The name of John Hampden stands out in the history of the English-speaking people, admired and unquestioned. He was neither a great statesman, nor a great soldier; he was not a brilliant orator, nor a famous writer. He fell bravely in an unimportant skirmish at Chalgrove Field, fighting for freedom and what he believed to be right. Yet he fills a great place in the past, both for what he did and what he was, and the reason for this is of high importance. John Hampden was a gentleman, with all the advantages that the accidents of birth could give. He was rich, educated, well born, of high traditions. English civilization of that day could produce nothing better. The memorable fact is that, when the time came for the test, he did not fail. He was a type of what was best among the English people, and when the call sounded, he was ready. He was brave, honest, high-minded, and he gave all, even his life, to his country. In the hour of need, the representative of what was best and most fortunate in England was put to the touch, and proved to be current gold. All men knew what that meant, and Hampden's memory is one of the glories of the English-speaking people.

Charles Lowell has the same meaning for us when rightly understood. He had all that birth, breeding, education, and tradition could give. The resources of our American life and civilization could produce nothing better. How would he and such men as he stand the great ordeal when it came? If wealth, education, and breeding were to result in a class who could only carp and criticize, accumulate money, give way to self-indulgence, and cherish low foreign ideals, then would it have appeared that there was a radical unsoundness in our society, refinement would have been proved to be weakness, and the highest education would have been shown to be a curse, rather than a blessing. But Charles Lowell, and hundreds of others like him, in greater or less degree, all over the land, met the great test and emerged triumphant. The Harvard men may be taken as fairly representing the colleges and universities of America. Harvard had, in 1860, 4157 living graduates, and 823 students, presumably over eighteen years old. Probably 3000 of her students and graduates were of military age, and not physically disqualified for military service. Of this number, 1230 entered the Union army or navy.

One hundred and fifty-six died in service, and 67 were killed in action.

Many did not go who might have gone, unquestionably, but the record is a noble one. Nearly one man of every two Harvard men came forward to serve his country when war was at our gates, and this proportion holds true, no doubt, of the other universities of the North.

It is well for the country, well for learning, well for our civilization, that such a record was made at such a time. Charles Lowell, and those like him, showed, once for all, that the men to whom fortune had been kindest were capable of the noblest patriotism, and shrank from no sacrifices. They taught the lesson which can never be heard too often—that the man to whom the accidents of birth and fortune have given most is the man who owes most to his country. If patriotism should exist anywhere, it should be strongest with such men as these, and their service should be ever ready. How nobly Charles Lowell in this spirit answered the great question, his life and death, alike victorious, show to all men.

SHERIDAN AT CEDAR CREEK

Inspired repulsed battalions to engage,
And taught the doubtful battle where to rage.

—ADDISON.

SHERIDAN AT CEDAR CREEK

General Sheridan took command of the Army of the Shenandoah in August, 1864. His coming was the signal for aggressive fighting, and for a series of brilliant victories over the rebel army. He defeated Early at Winchester and again at Fisher's Hill, while General Torbert whipped Rosser in a subsequent action, where the rout of the rebels was so complete that the fight was known as the "Woodstock races." Sheridan's plan after this was to terminate his campaign north of Staunton, and, returning thence, to desolate the Valley, so as to make it untenable for the Confederates, as well as useless as a granary or storehouse, and then move the bulk of his army through Washington, and unite them with General Grant in front of Petersburg. Grant, however, and the authorities at Washington, were in favor of Sheridan's driving Early into Eastern Virginia, and following up that line, which Sheridan himself believed to be a false move. This important matter was in debate until October 16, when Sheridan, having left the main body of his army at Cedar Creek under General Wright, determined to go to Washington, and discuss the question personally with General Halleck and the Secretary of War. He reached Washington on the morning of the 17th about eight o'clock, left there at twelve; and got back to Martinsburg the same night about dark. At Martinsburg he spent the night, and the next day, with his escort, rode to Winchester, reaching that point between three and four o'clock in the afternoon of the 18th. He there heard that all was quiet at Cedar Creek and along the front, and went to bed, expecting to reach his headquarters and join the army the next day.

About six o'clock, on the morning of the 19th, it was reported to him that artillery firing could be heard in the direction of Cedar Creek, but as the sound was stated to be irregular and fitful, he thought it only a skirmish. He, nevertheless, arose at once, and had just finished dressing when another officer came in, and reported that the firing was still going on in the same direction, but that it did not sound like a general battle. Still Sheridan was uneasy, and, after breakfasting, mounted his horse between eight and nine o'clock, and rode slowly through Winchester. When he reached the edge of the town he halted a moment, and then heard the firing of artillery in an unceasing roar.

He now felt confident that a general battle was in progress, and, as he rode forward, he was convinced, from the rapid increase of the sound, that his army was failing back. After he had crossed Mill Creek, just outside Winchester, and made the crest of the rise beyond the stream, there burst upon his view the spectacle of a panic-stricken army.

Hundreds of slightly wounded men, with hundreds

more unhurt, but demoralized, together with baggage wagons and trains, were all pressing to the rear, in hopeless confusion.

There was no doubt now that a disaster had occurred at the front. A fugitive told Sheridan that the army was broken and in full retreat, and that all was lost. Sheridan at once sent word to Colonel Edwards, commanding a brigade at Winchester, to stretch his troops across the valley, and stop all fugitives. His first idea was to make a stand there, but, as he rode along, a different plan flashed into his mind. He believed that his troops had great confidence in him, and he determined to try to restore their broken ranks, and, instead of merely holding the ground at Winchester, to rally his army, and lead them forward again to Cedar Creek. He had hardly made up his mind to this course, when news was brought to him that his headquarters at Cedar Creek were captured, and the troops dispersed. He started at once, with about twenty men as an escort, and rode rapidly to the front. As he passed along, the unhurt men, who thickly lined the road, recognized him, and, as they did so, threw up their hats, shouldered their muskets, and followed him as fast as they could on foot. His officers rode out on either side to tell the stragglers that the general had returned, and, as the news spread the retreating men in every direction rallied, and turned their faces toward the battle-field they had left.

In his memoirs, Sheridan says, in speaking of his ride through the retreating troops: "I said nothing, except to remark, as I rode among them 'If I had been with you this morning, this disaster would not have happened. We must face the other way. We will go back and recover our camp.'" Thus he galloped on over the twenty miles, with the men rallying behind him, and following him in ever increasing numbers. As he went by, the panic of retreat was replaced by the ardor of battle. Sheridan had not overestimated the power of enthusiasm or his own ability to rouse it to fighting pitch. He pressed steadily on to the front, until at last he came up to Getty's division of the 6th Corps, which, with the cavalry, were the only troops who held their line and were resisting the enemy.

Getty's division was about a mile north of Middletown on some slightly rising ground, and were skirmishing with the enemy's pickets. Jumping a rail fence, Sheridan rode to the crest of the hill, and, as he took off his hat, the men rose up from behind the barricades with cheers of recognition.

It is impossible to follow in detail Sheridan's actions from that moment, but he first brought up the 19th Corps and the two divisions of Wright to the front. He then communicated with Colonel Lowell, who was fighting near Middletown with his men dismounted, and asked him if he could hold on where he was, to which Lowell replied in the affirmative.

All this and many similar quickly-given orders consumed a great deal of time, but still the men were getting into line, and at last, seeing that the enemy were about to renew the attack, Sheridan rode along the line so that the men could all see him. He was received with the wildest enthusiasm as he rode by, and the spirit of the army was restored. The rebel attack was made shortly after noon, and was repulsed by General Emory.

This done, Sheridan again set to work to getting his line completely restored, while General Merritt charged and drove off an exposed battery of the Confederates. By half past three Sheridan was ready to attack.

The fugitives of the morning, whom he had rallied as he rode from Winchester, were again in their places, and the different divisions were all disposed in their proper positions. With the order to advance, the whole line pressed forward. The Confederates at first resisted stubbornly, and then began to retreat. On they went past Cedar Creek, and there, where the pike made a sharp turn to the west toward Fisher's Hill, Merritt and Custer fell on the flank of the retreating columns, and the rebel army fell back, routed and broken, up the Valley. The day had begun in rout and defeat; it ended in a great victory for the Union army.

How near we had been to a terrible disaster can be realized by recalling what had happened before the general galloped down from Winchester.

In Sheridan's absence, Early, soon after dawn, had made an unexpected attack on our army at Cedar Creek. Surprised by the assault, the national troops had given way in all directions, and a panic had set in.

Getty's division with Lowell's cavalry held on at Middletown, but, with this exception, the rout was complete. When Sheridan rode out of Winchester, he met an already beaten army. His first thought was the natural one to make a stand at Winchester and rally his troops about him there. His second thought was the inspiration of the great commander. He believed his men would rally as soon as they saw him. He believed that enthusiasm was one of the great weapons of war, and that this was the moment of all others when it might be used with decisive advantage. With this thought in his mind he abandoned the idea of forming his men at Winchester, and rode bareheaded through the fugitives, swinging his hat, straight for the front, and calling on his men as he passed to follow him. As the soldiers saw him, they turned and rushed after him. He had not calculated in vain upon the power of personal enthusiasm, but, at the same time, he did not rely upon any wild rush to save the day. The moment he reached the field of battle, he set to work with the coolness of a great soldier to make all the dispositions, first, to repel the enemy, and then to deliver an attack which could not be resisted. One division after another was rapidly brought into line and placed in position, the thin ranks filling fast with the soldiers who had recovered from their panic, and followed Sheridan and the black horse all the way down from Winchester. He had been already two hours on the field when, at noon, he rode along the line, again formed for battle.

Most of the officers and men then thought he had just come, while in reality it was his own rapid work which had put them in the line along which he was riding.

Once on the field of battle, the rush and hurry of the desperate ride from Winchester came to an end. First the line was reformed, then the enemy's assault was repulsed, and it was made impossible for them to again take the offensive. But Sheridan, undazzled by his brilliant success up to this point, did not mar his work by overhaste. Two hours more passed before he was ready, and then, when all was prepared, with his ranks established and his army ranged in position, he moved his whole line forward, and won one of the most brilliant battles of the war, having, by his personal power over his troops, and his genius in action, snatched a victory from a day which began in surprise, disaster, and defeat.

LIEUTENANT CUSHING AND THE RAM "ALBEMARLE"

God give us peace! Not such as lulls to sleep,
But sword on thigh, and brow with purpose knit!
And let our Ship of State to harbor sweep,
Her ports all up, her battle-lanterns lit,
And her leashed thunders gathering for their leap!

—LOWELL.

LIEUTENANT CUSHING AND THE RAM "ALBEMARLE"

The great Civil War was remarkable in many ways, but in no way more remarkable than for the extraordinary mixture of inventive mechanical genius and of resolute daring shown by the combatants. After the first year, when the contestants had settled down to real fighting, and the preliminary mob work was over, the battles were marked by their extraordinary obstinacy and heavy loss. In no European conflict since the close of the Napoleonic wars has the fighting been anything like as obstinate and as bloody as was the fighting in our own Civil War.

In addition to this fierce and dogged courage, this splendid fighting capacity, the contest also brought out the skilled inventive power of engineer and mechanician in a way that few other contests have ever done.

This was especially true of the navy. The fighting under and against Farragut and his fellow-admirals revolutionized naval warfare. The Civil War marks the break between the old style and the new. Terrible encounters took place when the terrible new engines of war were brought into action for the first time; and one of these encounters has given an example which, for heroic daring combined with cool intelligence, is unsurpassed in all time.

The Confederates showed the same skill and energy in building their great ironclad rams as the men of the Union did in building the monitors which were so often pitted against them. Both sides, but especially the Confederates, also used stationary torpedoes, and, on a number of occasions, torpedo-boats likewise. These torpedo-boats were sometimes built to go under the water. One such, after repeated failures, was employed by the Confederates, with equal gallantry and success, in sinking a Union sloop of war off Charleston harbor, the torpedo-boat itself going down to the bottom with its victim, all on board being drowned. The other type of torpedo-boat was simply a swift, ordinary steam-launch, operated above water.

It was this last type of boat which Lieutenant W. B. Cushing brought down to Albemarle Sound to use against the great Confederate ram Albemarle. The ram had been built for the purpose of destroying the Union blockading forces. Steaming down river, she had twice attacked the Federal gunboats, and in each case had sunk or disabled one or more of them, with little injury to herself. She had retired up the river again to lie at her wharf and refit. The gunboats had suffered so severely as to make it a certainty that when she came out again, thoroughly fitted to renew the attack, the wooden vessels would be destroyed; and while she was in existence, the Union vessels could not reduce the forts and coast towns. Just at this time Cushing came down from the North with his swift little torpedo-boat, an open launch, with a spar-rigged out in front, the torpedo being placed at the end. The crew of the launch consisted of fifteen men, Cushing being in command. He not only guided his craft, but himself handled the torpedo by means of two small ropes, one of which put it in place, while the other exploded it. The action of the torpedo was complicated, and it could not have been operated in a time of tremendous excitement save by a man of the utmost nerve and self-command; but Cushing had both. He possessed precisely that combination of reckless courage, presence of mind, and high mental capacity necessary to the man who leads a forlorn hope under peculiarly difficult circumstances.

On the night of October 27, 1864, Cushing slipped away from the blockading fleet, and steamed up river toward the wharf, a dozen miles distant, where the great ram lay. The Confederates were watchful to guard against surprise, for they feared lest their foes should try to destroy the ram before she got a chance to come down and attack them again in the Sound. She lay under the guns of a fort, with a regiment of troops ready at a moment's notice to turn out and defend her. Her own guns were kept always clear for action, and she was protected by a great boom of logs thrown out roundabout; of which last defense the Northerners knew nothing.

Cushing went up-stream with the utmost caution, and by good luck passed, unnoticed, a Confederate lookout below the ram.

About midnight he made his assault. Steaming quietly on through the black water, and feeling his way cautiously toward where he knew the town to be, he finally made out the loom of the Albemarle through the night, and at once drove at her. He was almost upon her before he was discovered; then the crew and the soldiers on the wharf opened fire, and, at the same moment, he was brought-to by the boom, the existence of which he had not known. The rifle balls were singing round him as he stood erect, guiding his launch, and he heard the bustle of the men aboard the ram, and the noise of the great guns as they were got ready.

Backing off, he again went all steam ahead, and actually surged over the slippery logs of the boom. Meanwhile, on the Albemarle the sailors were running to quarters, and the soldiers were swarming down to aid in her defense; and the droning bullets came always thicker through the dark night. Cushing still stood upright in his little craft, guiding and controlling her by voice and signal, while in his hands he kept the ropes which led to the torpedo. As the boat slid forward over the boom, he brought the torpedo full against the somber side of the huge ram, and instantly exploded it, almost at the same time that the pivot-gun of the ram, loaded with grape, was fired point-blank at him not ten yards off.

At once the ram settled, the launch sinking at the same moment, while Cushing and his men swam for their lives. Most of them sank or were captured, but Cushing reached mid-stream. Hearing something splashing in the darkness, he swam toward it, and found that it was one of his crew.

He went to his rescue, and they kept together for some time, but the sailor's strength gave out, and he finally sank. In the pitch darkness Cushing could form no idea where he was; and when, chilled through, and too exhausted to rise to his feet, he finally reached shore, shortly before dawn, he found that he had swum back and landed but a few hundred feet below the sunken ram. All that day he remained within easy musket-shot of where his foes were swarming about the fort and the great drowned ironclad. He hardly dared move, and until the afternoon he lay without food, and without protection from the heat or venomous insects.

Then he managed to slip unobserved into the dense swamp, and began to make his way to the fleet. Toward evening he came out on a small stream, near a camp of Confederate soldiers. They had moored to the bank a skiff, and, with equal stealth and daring, he managed to steal this and to paddle down-stream. Hour after hour he paddled on through the fading light, and then through the darkness. At last, utterly worn out, he found the squadron, and was picked up. At once the ships weighed; and they speedily captured every coast town and fort, for their dreaded enemy was no longer in the way. The fame of Cushing's deed went all over the North, and his name will stand forever among the brightest on the honor-roll of the American navy.

FARRAGUT AT MOBILE BAY

Ha, old ship, do they thrill,
The brave two hundred scars
You got in the river wars?
That were leeched with clamorous skill
(Surgery savage and hard),
At the Brooklyn Navy Yard.

* * *

How the guns, as with cheer and shout,
Our tackle-men hurled them out,
Brought up in the waterways . . .
As we fired, at the flash
'Twas lightning and black eclipse
With a bellowing sound and crash.

* * * *

The Dahlgrens are dumb,
Dumb are the mortars;
Never more shall the drum
Beat to colors and quarters—
The great guns are silent.

—HENRY HOWARD BROWNELL.

FARRAGUT AT MOBILE BAY

During the Civil War our navy produced, as it has always produced in every war, scores of capable officers, of brilliant single-ship commanders, of men whose daring courage made them fit leaders in any hazardous enterprise. In this respect the Union seamen in the Civil War merely lived up to the traditions of their service. In a service with such glorious memories it was a difficult thing to establish a new record in feats of personal courage or warlike address. Biddle, in the Revolutionary War, fighting his little frigate against a ship of the line until she blew up with all on board, after inflicting severe loss on her huge adversary; Decatur, heading the rush of the boarders in the night attack when they swept the wild Moorish pirates from the decks of their anchored prize; Lawrence, dying with the words on his lips, "Don't give up the ship"; and Perry, triumphantly steering his bloody sloop-of-war to victory with the same words blazoned on his banner—men like these, and like their fellows, who won glory in desperate conflicts with the regular warships and heavy privateers of England and France, or with the corsairs of the Barbary States, left behind a reputation which was hardly to be dimmed, though it might be emulated, by later feats of mere daring.

But vital though daring is, indispensable though desperate personal prowess and readiness to take chances are to the make-up of a fighting navy, other qualities are needed in addition to fit a man for a place among the great sea-captains of all time. It was the good fortune of the navy in the Civil War to produce one admiral of renown, one peer of all the mighty men who have ever waged war on the ocean. Farragut was not only the greatest admiral since Nelson, but, with the sole exception of Nelson, he was as great an admiral as ever sailed the broad or the narrow seas.

David Glasgow Farragut was born in Tennessee. He was appointed to the navy while living in Louisiana, but when the war came he remained loyal to the Union flag. This puts him in the category of those men who deserved best of their country in the Civil War; the men who were Southern by birth, but who stood loyally by the Union; the men like General Thomas of Virginia, and like Farragut's own flag-captain at the battle of Mobile Bay, Drayton of South Carolina. It was an easy thing in the North to support the Union, and it was a double disgrace to be, like Vallandigham and the Copperheads, against it; and in the South there were a great multitude of men, as honorable as they were brave, who, from the best of motives, went with their States when they seceded, or even advocated secession. But the highest and loftiest patriots, those who deserved best of the whole country, were the men from the South who possessed such heroic courage, and such lofty fealty to the high ideal of the Union, that they stood by the flag when their fellows deserted it, and unswervingly followed a career devoted to the cause of the whole nation and of the whole people. Among all those who fought in this, the greatest struggle for righteousness which the present century has seen, these men stand preeminent; and among them Farragut stands first. It was his good fortune that by his life he offered an example, not only of patriotism, but of supreme skill and daring in his profession. He belongs to that class of commanders who possess in the highest degree the qualities of courage and daring, of readiness to assume responsibility, and of willingness to run great risks; the qualities without which no commander, however cautious and able, can ever become really great. He possessed also the unwearied capacity for taking thought in advance, which enabled him to prepare for victory before the day of battle came; and he added to this an inexhaustible fertility of resource and presence of mind under no matter what strain.

His whole career should be taught every American schoolboy, for when that schoolboy becomes a voter he should have learned the lesson that the United States, while it ought not to become an overgrown military power, should always have a first-class navy, formidable from the number of its ships, and formidable still more from the excellence of the individual ships and the high character of the officers and men.

Farragut saw the war of 1812, in which, though our few frigates and sloops fought some glorious actions, our coasts were blockaded and insulted, and the Capitol at Washington burned, because our statesmen and our people had been too short-sighted to build a big fighting navy; and Farragut was able to perform his great feats on the Gulf coast because, when the Civil War broke out, we had a navy which, though too small in point of numbers, was composed of ships as good as any afloat.

Another lesson to be learned by a study of his career is that no man in a profession so highly technical as that of the navy can win a great success unless he has been brought up in and specially trained for that profession, and has devoted his life to the work. This fact was made plainly evident in the desperate hurly-burly of the night battle with the Confederate flotilla below New Orleans—the incidents of this hurly-burly being, perhaps, best described by the officer who, in his report of his own share in it, remarked that "all sorts of things happened." Of the Confederate rams there were two, commanded by trained officers formerly in the United States navy, Lieutenants Kennon and Warley. Both of these men handled their little vessels with remarkable courage, skill, and success, fighting them to the last, and inflicting serious and heavy damage upon the Union fleet. The other vessels of the flotilla were commanded by men who had not been in the regular navy, who were merely Mississippi River captains, and the like. These men were, doubtless, naturally as brave as any of the regular officers; but, with one or two exceptions, they failed ignobly in the time of trial, and showed a fairly startling contrast with the regular naval officers beside or against whom they fought. This is a fact which may well be pondered by the ignorant or unpatriotic people who believe that the United States does not need a navy, or that it can improvise one, and improvise officers to handle it, whenever the moment of need arises.

When a boy, Farragut had sailed as a midshipman on the Essex in her famous cruise to the South Pacific, and lived through the murderous fight in which, after losing three fifths of her crew, she was captured by two British vessels. Step by step he rose in his profession, but never had an opportunity of distinguishing himself until, when he was sixty years old, the Civil War broke out. He was then made flag officer of the Gulf squadron; and the first success which the Union forces met with in the southwest was scored by him, when one night he burst the iron chains which the Confederates had stretched across the Mississippi, and, stemming the swollen flood with his splendidly-handled steam-frigates, swept past the forts, sank the rams and gunboats that sought to bar his path, and captured the city of New Orleans. After further exciting service on the Mississippi, service in which he turned a new chapter in the history of naval warfare by showing the possibilities of heavy seagoing vessels when used on great rivers, he again went back to the Gulf, and, in the last year of the war, was allotted the task of attempting the capture of Mobile, the only important port still left open to the Confederates.

In August, 1864, Farragut was lying with his fleet off

Mobile Bay. For months he had been eating out his heart while undergoing the wearing strain of the blockade; sympathizing, too, with every detail of the doubtful struggle on land. "I get right sick, every now and then, at the bad news," he once wrote home; and then again, "The victory of the Kearsarge over the Alabama raised me up; I would sooner have fought that fight than any ever fought on the ocean." As for himself, all he wished was a chance to fight, for he had the fighting temperament, and he knew that, in the long run, an enemy can only be beaten by being out-fought, as well as out-maneuvered. He possessed a splendid self-confidence, and scornfully threw aside any idea that he would be defeated, while he utterly refused to be daunted by the rumors of the formidable nature of the defenses against which he was to act. "I mean to be whipped or to whip my enemy, and not to be scared to death," he remarked in speaking of these rumors.

The Confederates who held Mobile used all their skill in preparing for defense, and all their courage in making that defense good. The mouth of the bay was protected by two fine forts, heavily armed, Morgan and Gaines. The winding channels were filled with torpedoes, and, in addition, there was a flotilla consisting of three gunboats, and, above all, a big ironclad ram, the Tennessee, one of the most formidable vessels then afloat. She was not fast, but she carried six high-power rifled guns, and her armor was very powerful, while, being of light draft, she could take a position where Farragut's deep-sea ships could not get at her. Farragut made his attack with four monitors,—two of them, the Tecumseh and Manhattan, of large size, carrying 15-inch guns, and the other two, the Winnebago and Chickasaw, smaller and lighter, with 11-inch guns,—and the wooden vessels, fourteen in number. Seven of these were big sloops-of-war, of the general type of Farragut's own flagship, the Hartford. She was a screw steamer, but was a full-rigged ship likewise, with twenty-two 9-inch shell guns, arranged in broadside, and carrying a crew of three hundred men. The other seven were light gunboats. When Farragut prepared for the assault, he arranged to make the attack with his wooden ships in double column. The seven most powerful were formed on the right, in line ahead, to engage Fort Morgan, the heaviest of the two forts, which had to be passed close inshore to the right. The light vessels were lashed each to the left of one of the heavier ones. By this arrangement each pair of ships was given a double chance to escape, if rendered helpless by a shot in the boiler or other vital part of the machinery. The heaviest ships led in the fighting column, the first place being taken by the Brooklyn and her gunboat consort, while the second position was held by Farragut himself in the Hartford, with the little Metacomet lashed alongside. He waited to deliver the attack until the tide and the wind should be favorable, and made all his preparations with the utmost care and thoughtfulness.

Preeminently a man who could inspire affection in others, both the officers and men of the fleet regarded him with fervent loyalty and absolute trust.

The attack was made early on the morning of August 5. Soon after midnight the weather became hot and calm, and at three the Admiral learned that a light breeze had sprung up from the quarter he wished, and he at once announced, "Then we will go in this morning." At daybreak he was at breakfast when the word was brought that the ships were all lashed in couples. Turning quietly to his captain, he said, "Well, Drayton, we might as well get under way;" and at half-past six the monitors stood down to their stations, while the column of wooden ships was formed, all with the United States flag hoisted, not only at the peak, but also at every masthead. The four monitors, trusting in their iron sides, steamed in between the wooden ships and the fort. Every man in every craft was thrilling with the fierce excitement of battle; but in the minds of most there lurked a vague feeling of unrest over one danger. For their foes who fought in sight, for the forts, the gunboats, and, the great ironclad ram, they cared nothing; but all, save the very boldest, were at times awed, and rendered uneasy by the fear of the hidden and the unknown. Danger which is great and real, but which is shrouded in mystery, is always very awful; and the ocean veterans dreaded the torpedoes—the mines of death—which lay, they knew not where, thickly scattered through the channels along which they were to thread their way.

The tall ships were in fighting trim, with spars housed, and canvas furled. The decks were strewn with sawdust; every man was in his place; the guns were ready, and except for the song of the sounding-lead there was silence in the ships as they moved forward through the glorious morning. It was seven o'clock when the battle began, as the Tecumseh, the leading monitor, fired two shots at the fort. In a few minutes Fort Morgan was ablaze with the flash of her guns, and the leading wooden vessels were sending back broadside after broadside. Farragut stood in the port main-rigging, and as the smoke increased he gradually climbed higher, until he was close by the maintop, where the pilot was stationed for the sake of clearer vision. The captain, fearing lest by one of the accidents of battle the great admiral should lose his footing, sent aloft a man with a lasher, and had a turn or two taken around his body in the shrouds, so that he might not fall if wounded; for the shots were flying thick.

At first the ships used only their bow guns, and the Confederate ram, with her great steel rifles, and her three consorts, taking station where they could rake the advancing fleet, caused much loss. In twenty minutes after the opening of the fight the ships of the van were fairly abreast of the fort, their guns leaping and thundering; and under the weight of their terrific fire that of the fort visibly slackened. All was now uproar and slaughter, the smoke drifting off in clouds. The decks were reddened and ghastly with blood, and the wreck of flying splinters drove across them at each discharge. The monitor Tecumseh alone was silent. After firing the first two shots, her commander, Captain Craven, had loaded his two big guns with steel shot, and, thus prepared, reserved himself for the Confederate ironclad, which he had set his heart upon taking or destroying single-handed. The two columns of monitors and the wooden ships lashed in pairs were now approaching the narrowest part of the channel, where the torpedoes lay thickest; and the guns of the vessels fairly overbore and quelled the fire from the fort. All was well, provided only the two columns could push straight on without hesitation; but just at this moment a terrible calamity befell the leader of the monitors. The Tecumseh, standing straight for the Tennessee, was within two hundred yards of her foe, when a torpedo suddenly exploded beneath her. The monitor was about five hundred yards from the Hartford, and from the maintop Farragut, looking at her, saw her reel violently from side to side, lurch heavily over, and go down headforemost, her screw revolving wildly in the air as she disappeared.

Captain Craven, one of the gentlest and bravest of men, was in the pilot-house with the pilot at the time. As she sank, both rushed to the narrow door, but there was time for only one to get out. Craven was ahead, but drew to one side, saying, "After you, pilot." As the pilot leaped through, the water rushed in, and Craven and all his crew, save two men, settled to the bottom in their iron coffin.

None of the monitors were awed or daunted by the fate of their consort, but drew steadily onward. In the bigger monitors the captains, like the crews, had remained within the iron walls; but on the two light crafts the commanders had found themselves so harassed by their cramped quarters, that they both stayed outside on the deck. As these two steamed steadily ahead, the men on the flagship saw Captain Stevens, of the Winnebago, pacing calmly, from turret to turret, on his unwieldy iron craft, under the full fire of the fort. The captain of the Chickasaw, Perkins, was the youngest commander in the fleet, and as he passed the Hartford, he stood on top of the turret, waving his hat and dancing about in wildest excitement and delight.

But, for a moment, the nerve of the commander of the Brooklyn failed him. The awful fate of the Tecumseh and the sight of a number of objects in the channel ahead, which seemed to be torpedoes, caused him to hesitate. He stopped his ship, and then backed water, making sternway to the Hartford, so as to stop her also. It was the crisis of the fight and the crisis of Farragut's career. The column was halted in a narrow channel, right under the fire of the forts. A few moments' delay and confusion, and the golden chance would have been past, and the only question remaining would have been as to the magnitude of the disaster.

Ahead lay terrible danger, but ahead lay also triumph. It might be that the first ship to go through would be sacrificed to the torpedoes; it might be that others would be sacrificed; but go through the fleet must.

Farragut signaled to the Brooklyn to go ahead, but she still hesitated.

Immediately, the admiral himself resolved to take the lead. Backing hard he got clear of the Brooklyn, twisted his ship's prow short round, and then, going ahead fast, he dashed close under the Brooklyn's stern, straight at the line of buoys in the channel. As he thus went by the Brooklyn, a warning cry came from her that there were torpedoes ahead.

"Damn the torpedoes!" shouted the admiral; "go ahead, full speed;" and the Hartford and her consort steamed forward. As they passed between the buoys, the cases of the torpedoes were heard knocking against the bottom of the ship; but for some reason they failed to explode, and the Hartford went safely through the gates of Mobile Bay, passing the forts.

Farragut's last and hardest battle was virtually won. After a delay which allowed the flagship to lead nearly a mile, the Brooklyn got her head round, and came in, closely followed by all the other ships. The Tennessee strove to interfere with the wooden craft as they went in, but they passed, exchanging shots, and one of them striving to ram her, but inflicting only a glancing blow. The ship on the fighting side of the rear couple had been completely disabled by a shot through her boiler.

As Farragut got into the bay he gave orders to slip the gunboats, which were lashed to each of the Union ships of war, against the Confederate gunboats, one of which he had already disabled by his fire, so that she was run ashore and burnt. Jouett, the captain of the Metacomet, had been eagerly waiting this order, and had his men already standing at the hawsers, hatchet in hand. When the signal for the gunboats to chase was hoisted, the order to Jouett was given by word of mouth, and as his hearty "Aye, aye, sir," came in answer, the hatchets fell, the hawsers parted, and the Metacomet leaped forward in pursuit. A thick rainsquall came up, and rendered it impossible for the rear gunboats to know whither the Confederate flotilla had fled. When it cleared away, the watchers on the fleet saw that one of the two which were uninjured had slipped off to Fort Morgan, while the other, the Selma, was under the guns of the Metacomet, and was promptly carried by the latter.

Meanwhile the ships anchored in the bay, about four miles from Fort Morgan, and the crews were piped to breakfast; but almost as soon as it was begun, the lookouts reported that the great Confederate ironclad was steaming down, to do battle, single-handed, with the Union fleet. She was commanded by Buchanan, a very gallant and able officer, who had been on the Merrimac, and who trusted implicitly in his invulnerable sides, his heavy rifle guns, and his formidable iron beak. As the ram came on, with splendid courage, the ships got under way, while Farragut sent word to the monitors to attack the Tennessee at once. The fleet surgeon, Palmer, delivered these orders. In his diary he writes, "I came to the Chickasaw; happy as my friend Perkins habitually is, I thought he would turn a somerset with joy, when I told him, 'The admiral wants you to go at once and fight the Tennessee.'"

At the same time, the admiral directed the wooden vessels to charge the ram, bow on, at full speed, as well as to attack her with their guns. The monitors were very slow, and the wooden vessels began the attack.

The first to reach the hostile ironclad was the Monongahela, which struck her square amidships; and five minutes later the Lackawanna, going at full speed, delivered another heavy blow. Both the Union vessels fired such guns as would bear as they swung round, but the shots glanced harmlessly from the armor, and the blows of the ship produced no serious injury to the ram, although their own stems were crushed in several feet above and below the water line. The Hartford then struck the Tennessee, which met her bows on. The two antagonists scraped by, their port sides touching. As they rasped past, the Hartford's guns were discharged against the ram, their muzzles only half a dozen feet distant from her iron-clad sides; but the shot made no impression. While the three ships were circling to repeat the charge, the Lackawanna ran square into the flagship, cutting the vessel down to within two feet of the water. For a moment the ship's company thought the vessel sinking, and almost as one man they cried: "Save the admiral! Get the admiral on board the Lackawanna." But Farragut, leaping actively into the chains, saw that the ship was in no present danger, and ordered her again to be headed for the Tennessee. Meanwhile, the monitors had come up, and the battle raged between them and the great ram. Like the rest of the Union fleet, they carried smoothbores, and their shot could not break through her iron plates; but by sustained and continuous hammering, her frame could be jarred and her timbers displaced. Two of the monitors had been more or less disabled already, but the third, the Chickasaw, was in fine trim, and Perkins got her into position under the stern of the Tennessee, just after the latter was struck by the Hartford; and there he stuck to the end, never over fifty yards distant, and keeping up a steady rapping of 11-inch shot upon the iron walls, which they could not penetrate, but which they racked and shattered. The Chickasaw fired fifty-two times at her antagonist, shooting away the exposed rudder-chains and the smokestack, while the commander of the ram, Buchanan, was wounded by an iron splinter which broke his leg. Under the hammering, the Tennessee became helpless. She could not be steered, and was unable to bring a gun to bear, while many of the shutters of the ports were jammed. For twenty minutes she had not fired a shot. The wooden vessels were again bearing down to ram her; and she hoisted the white flag.

Thus ended the battle of Mobile Bay, Farragut's crowning victory. Less than three hours elapsed from the time that Fort Morgan fired its first gun to the moment when the Tennessee hauled down her flag. Three hundred and thirty-five men had been killed or wounded in the fleet, and one vessel, the Tecumseh, had gone down; but the Confederate flotilla was destroyed, the bay had been entered, and the forts around it were helpless to do anything further. One by one they surrendered, and the port of Mobile was thus sealed against blockade runners, so that the last source of communication between the Confederacy and the outside world was destroyed. Farragut had added to the annals of the Union the page which tells of the greatest sea-fight in our history.

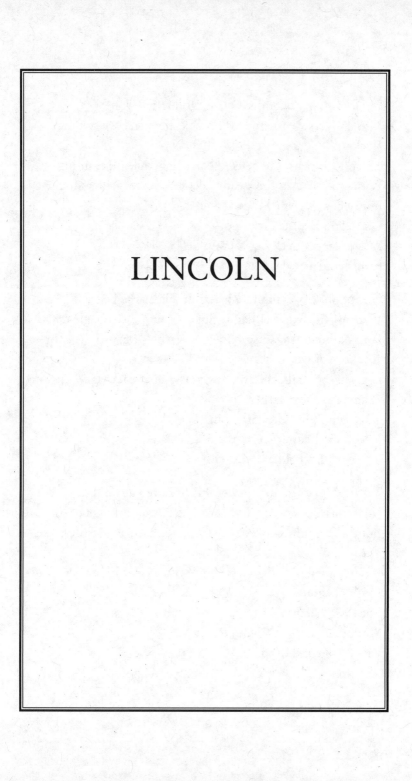

LINCOLN

O captain. My captain. Our fearful trip is done;
The ship has weathered every rack, the prize we sought is
  won;
The port is near, the bells I hear, the people all exulting,
While follow eyes the steady keel, the vessel grim and daring:
But O heart! Heart! Heart!
Leave you not the little spot,
Where on the deck my captain lies,
Fallen cold and dead.

O captain. My captain. Rise up and hear the bells;
Rise up—for you the flag is flung—for you the bugle trills;
For you bouquets and ribbon'd wreaths—for you the shores
  a-crowding;
For you they call, the swaying mass, their eager faces turning;
O captain. Dear father.
This arm I push beneath you;
It is some dream that on the deck,
You've fallen cold and dead.

My captain does not answer, his lips are pale and still;
My father does not feel my arm, he has no pulse nor will:
But the ship, the ship is anchor'd safe, its voyage closed and
  done;
From fearful trip, the victor ship, comes in with object won:
Exult O shores, and ring, O bells.
But I with silent tread,
Walk the spot the captain lies,
Fallen cold and dead.

—WALT WHITMAN.

LINCOLN

As Washington stands to the Revolution and the establishment of the government, so Lincoln stands as the hero of the mightier struggle by which our Union was saved. He was born in 1809, ten years after Washington, his work done had been laid to rest at Mount Vernon. No great man ever came from beginnings which seemed to promise so little.

Lincoln's family, for more than one generation, had been sinking, instead of rising, in the social scale. His father was one of those men who were found on the frontier in the early days of the western movement, always changing from one place to another, and dropping a little lower at each remove. Abraham Lincoln was born into a family who were not only poor, but shiftless, and his early days were days of ignorance, and poverty, and hard work. Out of such inauspicious surroundings, he slowly and painfully lifted himself. He gave himself an education, he took part in an Indian war, he worked in the fields, he kept a country store, he read and studied, and, at last, he became a lawyer. Then he entered into the rough politics of the newly-settled State. He grew to be a leader in his county, and went to the legislature. The road was very rough, the struggle was very hard and very bitter, but the movement was always upward.

At last he was elected to Congress, and served one term in Washington as a Whig with credit, but without distinction. Then he went back to his law and his politics in Illinois. He had, at last, made his position.

All that was now needed was an opportunity, and that came to him in the great anti-slavery struggle.

Lincoln was not an early Abolitionist. His training had been that of a regular party man, and as a member of a great political organization, but he was a lover of freedom and justice. Slavery, in its essence, was hateful to him, and when the conflict between slavery and freedom was fairly joined, his path was clear before him. He took up the antislavery cause in his own State and made himself its champion against Douglas, the great leader of the Northern Democrats. He stumped Illinois in opposition to Douglas, as a candidate for the Senate, debating the question which divided the country in every part of the State. He was beaten at the election, but, by the power and brilliancy of his speeches, his own reputation was made. Fighting the anti-slavery battle within constitutional lines, concentrating his whole force against the single point of the extension of slavery to the Territories, he had made it clear that a new leader had arisen in the cause of freedom. From Illinois his reputation spread to the East, and soon after his great debate he delivered a speech in New York which attracted wide attention.

At the Republican convention of 1856, his name was one of those proposed for vice-president.

When 1860 came, he was a candidate for the first place on the national ticket. The leading candidate was William H. Seward, of New York, the most conspicuous man of the country on the Republican side, but the convention, after a sharp struggle, selected Lincoln, and then the great political battle came at the polls. The Republicans were victorious, and, as soon as the result of the voting was known, the South set to work to dissolve the Union. In February Lincoln made his way to Washington, at the end coming secretly from Harrisburg to escape a threatened attempt at assassination, and on March 4, 1861 assumed the presidency.

No public man, no great popular leader, ever faced a more terrible situation. The Union was breaking, the Southern States were seceding, treason was rampant in Washington, and the Government was bankrupt. The country knew that Lincoln was a man of great capacity in debate, devoted to the cause of antislavery and to the maintenance of the Union. But what his ability was to deal with the awful conditions by which he was surrounded, no one knew. To follow him through the four years of civil war which ensued is, of course, impossible here. Suffice it to say that no greater, no more difficult, task has ever been faced by any man in modern times, and no one ever met a fierce trial and conflict more successfully.

Lincoln put to the front the question of the Union,

and let the question of slavery drop, at first, into the background. He used every exertion to hold the border States by moderate measures, and, in this way, prevented the spread of the rebellion. For this moderation, the antislavery extremists in the North assailed him, but nothing shows more his far-sighted wisdom and strength of purpose than his action at this time. By his policy at the beginning of his administration, he held the border States, and united the people of the North in defense of the Union.

As the war went on, he went on, too. He had never faltered in his feelings about slavery. He knew, better than any one, that the successful dissolution of the Union by the slave power meant, not only the destruction of an empire, but the victory of the forces of barbarism. But he also saw, what very few others at the moment could see, that, if he was to win, he must carry his people with him, step by step. So when he had rallied them to the defense of the Union, and checked the spread of secession in the border States, in the autumn of 1862 he announced that he would issue a proclamation freeing the slaves.

The extremists had doubted him in the beginning, the conservative and the timid doubted him now, but when the Emancipation Proclamation was issued, on January 1, 1863, it was found that the people were with him in that, as they had been with him when he staked everything upon the maintenance of the Union. The war went on to victory, and in 1864 the people showed at the polls that they were with the President, and reelected him by overwhelming majorities. Victories in the field went hand in hand with success at the ballot-box, and, in the spring of 1865, all was over. On April 9, 1865, Lee surrendered at Appomattox, and five days later, on April 14, a miserable assassin crept into the box at the theater where the President was listening to a play, and shot him. The blow to the country was terrible beyond words, for then men saw, in one bright flash, how great a man had fallen.

Lincoln died a martyr to the cause to which he had given his life, and both life and death were heroic. The qualities which enabled him to do his great work are very clear now to all men. His courage and his wisdom, his keen perception and his almost prophetic foresight, enabled him to deal with all the problems of that distracted time as they arose around him. But he had some qualities, apart from those of the intellect, which were of equal importance to his people and to the work he had to do. His character, at once strong and gentle, gave confidence to every one, and dignity to his cause. He had an infinite patience, and a humor that enabled him to turn aside many difficulties which could have been met in no other way. But most important of all was the fact that he personified a great sentiment, which ennobled and uplifted his people, and made them capable of the patriotism which fought the war and saved the Union. He carried his people with him, because he knew instinctively, how they felt and what they wanted. He embodied, in his own person, all their highest ideals, and he never erred in his judgment.

He is not only a great and commanding figure among the great statesmen and leaders of history, but he personifies, also, all the sadness and the pathos of the war, as well as its triumphs and its glories. No words that any one can use about Lincoln can, however, do him such justice as his own, and I will close this volume with two of Lincoln's speeches, which show what the war and all the great deeds of that time meant to him, and through which shines, the great soul of the man himself. On November 19, 1863, he spoke as follows at the dedication of the National cemetery on the battle-field of Gettysburg:

Fourscore and seven years ago our fathers brought forth on this continent a new nation, conceived in liberty, and dedicated to the proposition that all men are created equal.

Now we are engaged in a great civil war, testing whether that nation, or any nation so conceived and so dedicated, can long endure. We are met on a great battle-field of that war. We have come to dedicate a portion of that field as a final resting place for those who here gave their lives that that nation might live. It is altogether fitting and proper that we should do this.

But in a larger sense, we cannot dedicate—we cannot consecrate—we cannot hallow—this ground. The brave men, living and dead, who struggled here, have consecrated it far above our poor power to add or detract. The world will little note or long remember what we say here, but it can never forget what they did here. It is for us, the living, rather, to be dedicated here to the unfinished work which they who have fought here, have thus far so nobly advanced. It is rather for us to be here dedicated to the great task remaining before us—that from the honored dead we take increased devotion to that cause for which they gave the last full measure of devotion; that we here highly resolve that these dead shall not have died in vain; that this nation, under God, shall have a new birth of freedom; and that government of the people, by the people, for the people, shall not perish from the earth.

On March 4, 1865, when he was inaugurated the second time, he made the following address:

Fellow-Countrymen: At this second appearing to take the oath of presidential office, there is less occasion for an extended address than there was at the first. Then a statement, somewhat in detail, of a course to be pursued, seemed proper. Now, at the expiration of four years, during which public declarations have been constantly called forth on every point and phase of the great contest which still absorbs the attention and engrosses the energies of the nation, little that is new could be presented. The progress of our arms, upon which all else chiefly depends, is as well known to the public as to myself; and it is, I trust, reasonably satisfactory and encouraging to all. With high hope for the future, no prediction in regard to it is ventured.

On the occasion corresponding to this four years ago, all thoughts were anxiously directed to an impending civil war. All dreaded it—all sought to avert it. While the inaugural address was being delivered from this place, devoted altogether to saving the Union without war, insurgent agents were in the city seeking to destroy it without war—seeking to dissolve the Union, and divide effects, by negotiation. Both parties deprecated war; but one of them would make war rather than let it perish. And the war came.

One eighth of the whole population were colored slaves, not distributed generally over the Union, but localized in the southern part of it.

These slaves constituted a peculiar and powerful interest. All knew that this interest was, somehow, the cause of the war. To strengthen, perpetuate, and extend this interest was the object for which the insurgents would rend the Union, even by war; while the government claimed no right to do more than to restrict the Territorial enlargement of it. Neither party expected for the war the magnitude or the duration which it has already attained. Neither anticipated that the cause of the conflict might cease with, or even before, the conflict itself should cease.

Each looked for an easier triumph, and a result less fundamental and astounding. Both read the same Bible, and pray to the same God; and each invokes his aid against the other. It may seem strange that any man should dare to ask a just God's assistance in wringing their bread from the sweat of other men's faces; but let us judge not, that we be not judged. The prayers of both could not be answered that of neither has been answered fully.

The Almighty has his own purposes. "Woe unto the world because of offenses, for it must needs be that offenses come; but woe to that man by whom the offense cometh." If we shall suppose that American slavery is one of those offenses which, in the providence of God, must needs come, but which, having continued through his appointed time, he now wills to remove, and that he gives to both North and South this terrible war, as the woe due to those by whom the offenses come, shall we discern therein any departure from those divine attributes which the believers in a living God always ascribe to him? Fondly do we hope—fervently do we pray—that this mighty scourge of war may speedily pass away. Yet, if God wills that it continue until all the wealth piled by the bondman's two hundred and fifty years of unrequited toil shall be sunk, and until every drop of blood drawn with the lash shall be paid by another drawn with the sword, as was said three thousand years ago, so still it must be said,

"The judgments of the Lord are true and righteous altogether."

With malice toward none; with charity for all; with firmness in the right, as God gives us to see the right, let us strive on to finish the work we are in; to bind up the nation's wounds; to care for him who shall have borne the battle, and for his widow, and his orphan—to do all which may achieve and cherish a just, a lasting, peace among ourselves and with all nations.

YOUR
HERO TALES

To wake the soul by tender strokes of art,
To raise the genius and to mend the heart,
To make mankind in conscious virtue bold,
Live o'er each scene, and be what they behold:

—ALEXANDER POPE.

YOUR HERO TALES

Henry Cabot Lodge and Teddy Roosevelt chose hero tales that inspired them and that they wanted young Americans to read and remember. They knew they were missing many great people and spent a lot of time selecting the 26 tales they wanted to share. Almost 150 years have passed since the death of their last hero, Abraham Lincoln. Since then, many more heroes and heroines have come along to serve their families, communities and country and to inspire us all.

The McConnell Center hopes you will use the pages that follow to record the names and stories of men and women whom you consider heroes from American history. May they help you remember American history and inspire you to great things in the years ahead.

Your Hero Tales

ABOUT THE AUTHORS

HENRY CABOT LODGE served in the United States Senate from 1893 until his death in 1924. He served as leader of the Republican Party in the Senate and is widely considered to have been the first *de facto* Majority Leader of that body. His was one of the most important voices in American foreign policy in the early 20th century, and his leadership against Woodrow Wilson's plan to join the League of Nations is credited with defeating that attempt at an international body. Though he supported an international organization to work for peace, he opposed what he took to be the plan's undermining of Congress's constitutional authority to declare war. Beyond his statesmanship, Lodge was also an accomplished scholar and writer. He edited the works of Alexander Hamilton and wrote important biographies of Hamilton, Daniel Webster and George Washington. Read more about Lodge's impressive life of diverse accomplishments in biographies and on the web.

THEODORE ROOSEVELT was the 26th President of the United States (1901–1909). He became president upon the assassination of President William McKinley and was himself shot in the chest while campaigning for office in 1912. He went on to deliver his speech with the bullet lodged in his chest and blood soaking through his shirt.

His opening lines of that speech are worthy of inclusion in a hero tale: "Ladies and gentlemen, I don't know whether you fully understand that I have just been shot; but it takes more than that to kill a Bull Moose." Among his many accomplishments, Roosevelt held numerous political positions, authored 18 books and won a Nobel Prize. Learn more about his adventures on safari, in the wilderness of America's west, exploring the Amazon and reforming American government in books and on the web.

MITCH MCCONNELL is the Republican Leader of the U.S. Senate and the longest serving U.S. Senator in Kentucky history. Born in Sheffield, Alabama, Senator McConnell moved with his family to Louisville as a boy, attended Louisville public schools, and graduated with honors from the University of Louisville College of Arts and Sciences, where he was student body president, and the University of Kentucky College of Law, where he was president of the Student Bar Association. Senator McConnell was judge-executive of Jefferson County, Kentucky, from 1978 until his swearing-in to the Senate in 1985. Senator McConnell served as Majority Whip in the 108th and 109th Congresses and Republican Leader in the 110th and 111th Congresses. Married to former U.S. Secretary of Labor Elaine L. Chao, Senator McConnell resides in Louisville.

About the Authors

GARY L. GREGG II holds the Mitch McConnell Chair in Leadership at the University of Louisville where he is also director of the McConnell Center. He has written or edited 10 books, including a volume about one of his greatest heroes, George Washington. He also writes a series of young adult novels (*The Sporran* and *The Iona Conspiracy*) that, in part, explore hero tales from Scottish history and whose contemporary hero is a young boy from Kentucky.

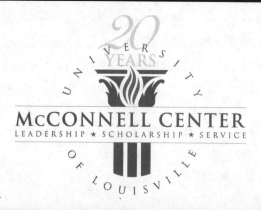

20 years of educational excellence

The McConnell Center was established in 1991 by U.S. Senator Mitch McConnell and the University of Louisville. McConnell, a 1964 graduate of the university, founded the Center based on his belief that "Kentucky's future depends on inspiring talented, motivated leaders."

The McConnell Center is dedicated to providing a nonpartisan, well-rounded education that encourages top undergraduates to become valued citizens and future leaders of the Commonwealth and the nation. The Center also facilitates public discussion on the major challenges of our time while encouraging an understanding of our shared past.

The McConnell Center hosts a public lecture series and coordinates the McConnell Scholars Program and Civic Education Program for Kentucky students and teachers. The Center is also proud to house the U.S. Senator Mitch McConnell and U.S. Secretary of Labor Elaine L. Chao Archives.

Visit **mcconnellcenter.org** to learn more.

McConnell Scholarships for Young Leaders

The McConnell Center is home to one of the most competitive and prestigious scholarship programs in Kentucky. Each year, the program attracts outstanding high school seniors from around the Commonwealth. Finalists take part in a two-day interview process. Ten students are then selected as McConnell Scholars and are awarded four-year scholarships to the University of Louisville.

McConnell Scholars receive tuition scholarships, have the chance to meet today's most influential leaders, interact with experts in a variety of fields from across the nation, intern in fields of their choice and travel the world. In its first 20 years, the Center has given nearly 200 students nearly $2.5 million in scholarship money, mentored them to compete for elite national scholarships for graduate school and helped them travel the world from the Highlands of Scotland to the most rural village of China.

Graduates of the program have gone on to further study at institutions such as Harvard Law School, Johns Hopkins University, Oxford University and Cambridge University in England. Though McConnell Scholars have a diversity of professional interests from medicine to legal studies, former students have also taken top positions in politics from the Governor's Mansion to the White House.

If you are an outstanding high school student leader, apply for the McConnell Scholars Program during the fall of your senior year. Where can a McConnell Scholarship take you?

Publications and Scholarship

The McConnell Center believes in the continuing importance of the printed word and the efficacy of first-rate academic scholarship. To enhance our dialogue on perennial topics, as well as the concerns of the moment, the Center publishes a variety of studies and research on topics ranging from the history of the Senate to the relevance of the Electoral College. Most of these are available in small quantities and for educational purposes.

Leadership, Government and History Institutes for Future Leaders

The McConnell Center regularly sponsors seminars, institutes and academies for young leaders in Kentucky. These programs bring high school students to Louisville, Ky., to interact with top scholars and explore contemporary issues and perennial concerns. The Center's signature "Young Leaders Academy" is a summer residential program for top students interested in deepening their understanding of American politics, the challenges of citizenship and the foundational ideas of the constitutional order.

Continuing Education for Teachers

The McConnell Center believes that America's future depends on educating our young people about our history and political institutions. Realizing our shared citizenship, the Center is dedicated to helping teachers impact the future by teaching our past. The Center regularly runs professional development programs for teachers in a variety of formats, from small seminars to week-long institutes.

Public Education Program

The McConnell Center's Distinguished Lecture Series has brought some of today's most important leaders to Louisville, Ky., to interact with students and speak to our community. These have included more than a dozen U.S. Senators, two Supreme Court Justices, five sitting or former Secretaries of State, two heads of foreign states, several ambassadors and Pulitzer Prize winning authors. The Center also regularly brings to campus some of today's most interesting authors, academics and experts from a variety of fields ranging from poetry to public policy. Conferences have been held on topics ranging from our Founding Fathers to Henry Clay to important moments in presidential history. All programs are open to the public and are usually free of charge.

★ ★ ★ ★ ★

THE SENATOR MITCH **MCCONNELL**
AND SECRETARY ELAINE L. **CHAO**
ARCHIVES

UNIVERSITY OF LOUISVILLE

Built around the careers of U.S. Senator Mitch McConnell and former U.S. Secretary of Labor Elaine L. Chao, the Civic Education Gallery of the McConnell-Chao Archives offers award-winning films, cutting-edge computer interactives and displays designed to educate visitors about American government, history and politics.

Visitors can:

★ *Take a computer-generated citizenship test*
★ *Watch and evaluate campaign commercials with noted experts Michael Barone and Jennifer Duffy*
★ *View an award-winning film on the history of the U.S. Senate narrated by Senator McConnell*
★ *View "The Promise of America," an-award winning film outlining Elaine Chao's rise from immigrant to member of the President's Cabinet*
★ *Learn essential lessons from American history and our experience under the U.S. Constitution*
★ *See awards, commendations, documents and other artifacts from the long careers of two of the most consequential Americans of the last two decades*

The gallery, located at the University of Louisville, is free and open to the public. Guided group tours are available.
Please call 502-852-8811 or visit mcconnellcenter.org.

McConnell Center Digital Library
An education at your fingertips

The McConnell Center provides a variety of educational and teaching materials online at **mcconnellcenter.org**.

Our popular iTunes U series features commentary and video from McConnell Center guest speakers. Digital books and reports are available for download.

Read our blog, "McConnell Center Life," to learn about the experiences of our 40 McConnell Scholars, a group of Kentucky's top undergraduate students who excel in leadership, scholarship and service.

Round out your digital experience and view our YouTube video collection, browse our Flickr photo gallery and follow us on Facebook.

The journey begins at **mcconnellcenter.org**.